This Book Will
Make You Calm

Dr Jessamy Hibberd
and
Jo Usmar

Quercus

Quercus Editions Ltd
55 Baker Street
7th Floor, South Block
London
W1U 8EW

First published in 2014

A CIP catalogue record for this book is available from the British Library

ISBN 978 1 84866 283 4
Printed in Great Britain by Clays Ltd, St Ives Plc

10 9 8 7 6 5 4 3 2 1

Designed for Quercus Editions Ltd by Peggy Sadler at Bookworx
www.bookworx.biz

Contents

A note from the authors

We live in ever-changing times and sometimes life can be tough. We're constantly being pulled in different directions and can struggle to cope with the pressure that we're put under by external factors and, most importantly, by ourselves. With greater choice comes greater responsibility and occasionally this can be a breeding ground for stress, unhappiness and self-doubt. There are very few people (if any at all) who feel they operate perfectly in their work, relationships and life in general. Most of us could use some help now and then – a nudge to show us how to improve our mood, to change our approach to life and to feel more content.

This series aims to help you understand why you feel, think and behave the way you do – and then gives you the tools to make positive changes. We're not fans of complicated medical jargon so we've tried to make everything accessible, relevant and entertaining as we know you'll want to see improvements as soon as possible. These concise, practical guides show you how to focus your thinking, develop coping strategies and learn practical techniques to face anything and everything in more positive and helpful ways.

We believe self-help doesn't have to be confusing, worthy or patronising. We draw on our professional experience and the latest research, using anecdotes and examples which we found helpful and hope you will too. Titles are split into particular areas of concern such as sleep, happiness, confidence and stress, so you can focus on the areas you'd most like to address.

Our books are based on a Cognitive Behavioural Therapy (CBT) framework. CBT is an incredibly successful treatment for a wide variety of issues and we're convinced it will enable you to cope with whatever you're facing.

Within the books you'll regularly come across diagrams called mind maps. They are easy to use and simple to understand. Based on CBT, mind maps show how your thoughts, behaviour and how you feel (both emotionally and physically) are all connected, breaking the problem down so it doesn't seem overwhelming, and laying out options for making changes.

There are exercises and checklists throughout, to guide you through the practical steps of altering how you feel. We'll make it easy to make these changes part of your routine because reading the theory is only going to get you so far. The only way to ensure you'll feel better long-term is to put everything you learn into practice and change how you experience your day-to-day life.

You can *choose* to feel better and these books will show you how.

Good luck! Let us know how you get on by contacting us on our website: www.jessamyandjo.com

Jessamy and Jo

Introduction

If you look up the word 'calm' in a dictionary, chances are you'll stumble across a phrase like 'the calm before the storm' or something else equally sea shanty-ish. This common analogy is a great way of describing not just what happens in nature, but also in our heads. Humans are built to experience both calm and stormy feelings, sliding back and forth across the emotional spectrum from despair to euphoria. Unfortunately our response to environmental, societal and psychological pressure is often to feel stressed, worried or anxious and we can end up becoming trapped in a whirlwind of tension. If someone feels this way regularly – or constantly – it can be hugely damaging to their health, both physically and mentally. If you're feeling panicky and anxious all the time, we'd put good money (hypothetically – we don't want to give you something else to worry about) on the fact that your physical health is suffering, your thoughts are mainly negative and you're behaving in a way that's often out of character.

Stress, anxiety and worry: three's a crowd

Many people commonly bunch rapid-heartbeat-knot-in-stomach emotions under the seemingly all-encompassing umbrella title of 'stress', when in reality stress, worry and anxiety are very different beasts. We explain their varying roles in much more detail in later chapters, but for now, suffice to say they all contribute to feeling like you're losing your grip on things.

Experiencing stress, anxiety and worry in life is totally natural. We're constantly put under pressure within our roles as friends, relatives, partners, parents, colleagues, neighbours, students, etc. We wear many different faces on a day-to-day basis and not only have to live according to our own measures of success, but those of society as a whole. Often the scale of what we're expected to achieve and how we're expected to act can feel frightening, leading us to question our ability to cope. The fact that we live in very demanding times was reflected by the 7 per cent rise in the number of hospital admissions for stress in England in the twelve months to May 2012 and the 44 per cent of Americans who said their stress levels had increased in the five years leading up to 2010. Stress affects everyone and feeling you can't cope can make life a struggle.

Stress, anxiety and worry can hugely affect your life, which is why it's so important to learn how to deal with issues and problems in a calm way. Life can feel out of control when you're under massive amounts of pressure, but you absolutely can wrestle it back. The good news is that there are loads of proactive steps you can take to feel calmer, to make your life more manageable and therefore happier – and this book will show you how.

Why choose this book?

We've both experienced stress, anxiety and worry ourselves and believe a book such as this could really have helped. We've tried to keep it as concise as possible so you won't get bogged down in confusing medical drivel that doesn't relate to you. If stress, anxiety and worry have been eating you up for a day, a week, a month or forever, please do give our strategies a shot. However, if your stress levels are seriously affecting your job or family life you also should consider visiting your

GP and getting things checked out in case you need more specialist help – but there's no harm in trying our techniques and strategies before, or as well as, taking that step. (We have included a list of resources at the back of the book.)

We're 100 per cent certain that *This Book Will Make You Calm* really will live up to its title, giving you the means to increase your ability to cope with the pressures of daily life. We've included tips and tools throughout that offer simple and effective ways of changing how you deal with both short and long term angst. You'll learn how to stop beating yourself up, how to ditch your futile quest for perfection (it doesn't exist by the way), and how to stop believing you're less than you are. In short, you'll learn how to enjoy your life.

How it all works

This is a really practical book – a manual on how to feel calmer. We recommend that you dedicate a bit of time and energy into fully absorbing everything and to trying out the strategies recommended. And while you can dip in and out of each chapter we'd encourage you to read them in numerical order as each one builds on the last.

The book is based around a Cognitive Behavioural Therapy (CBT) framework, which is explained in more detail in Chapter 2. It's a highly effective problem-focused approach that finds practical ways of managing the here and now. You'll learn a set of principles and techniques that will help you deal with on-going problems (and any new ones) and this new knowledge will stay with you for life.

How to get the most out of this book

✦ Try all of the strategies out, rather than just flicking through them.
   (The strategies are all identified by Ⓢ) These techniques are proven
   to work, we're not experimenting on you. If you invest time and
   energy into them they absolutely will change your life for the better.
   Some may suit you more than others, but by trying them all you'll
   give yourself the best possible shot at feeling calmer.

✦ Practise. If something doesn't work for you immediately, try again.
   As with anything, the more you practice the more familiar these
   new ways of thinking and behaving will become. Adopting positive
   new habits can take a while, but the more you use them the quicker
   they'll become second nature.

✦ Buy a new notebook to dedicate specifically to this book. Several
   of our strategies involve writing things down or drawing stuff out.
   It'll be motivational and practical to be able to flip back to things
   you've previously written and to see how far you've come. Also, the
   very act of writing things down aids memory and will make your
   determination to change more 'official' in your head.

We genuinely do believe that while stress, anxiety and worry are part
of everyday life, they don't have to rule your life. You can take control
and in doing so you'll feel happier, more confident and calmer.

Understanding Stress

Stress has many faces – many frustrating, frightening and panicky faces. Here we explain what stress is, its relationship to worry and anxiety and why it's affecting your life. Understanding stress is an integral step in learning how to manage it.

What are stress, anxiety and worry?

Your thoughts, behaviour, emotions and physical health are all intrinsically interlinked. For example, if you feel jealous, your thoughts will be negative, you might behave badly and physically your heart rate might speed up. Not one of these processes is more important than the other and there isn't one in particular that triggers everything else. It totally depends on the type of person you are and what situation you're in, i.e. you might think something negative which then prompts you to behave in a negative way, which in turn makes you feel bad and causes your body to physically tense up.

It's a big fat vicious circle:

Physicality
Heart racing, sweating,
nervous twitch, hand
wringing

Emotions
Anxious
Sad
Stressed

Behaviour
Become aggressive
or more tentative
Snap at people
Avoid social occasions

Thoughts
Worried, negative,
frightened

Stress, anxiety and worry

Stress: a response to a situation or event in which you're put under pressure. It affects you emotionally and physically and influences your thoughts and behaviour.

Anxiety: an emotion. In relation to stress it's a fear of failure or a perception of threat or danger.

Worry: a negative thought process about the future, i.e. 'what if ...?'

Example: Poppy's predicament

Scenario A: Poppy's daughter wakes up with a hideous cough – there's no way she can go to school. Poppy will have to stay at home and look after her, which is frustrating because she had an important meeting scheduled at the office. Poppy feels stressed because she's under pressure, but she's not anxious as she knows she can reschedule the meeting without any major repercussions.

Scenario B: Poppy's meeting is with an important international client who is only available for one day. She feels anxious about the pressure she's under (stress) as she's fearful about the ⋯⋮⋅

⋯∴ possible consequences of cancelling. This triggers worrying thoughts such as, 'What if he takes his business elsewhere? What if he thinks I'm unreliable? I can't afford to lose this client …' which could start to manifest themselves physically, perhaps through an increased heart rate, a knot in the pit of her stomach or shaking hands.

We're pretty sure everyone has been told to 'calm down' by a well-meaning, but intensely annoying person at some point. As far as advice goes it's pretty damn useless. There's no way you can just switch stress, anxiety and worry off and someone – no matter how well meaning – suggesting you can is only going to aggravate matters. However, there are practical ways of making things more manageable so the next time someone tells you to calm down you won't feel like hitting them.

Feeling stressed

Stress affects different people at different times and in different ways. Whatever causes people to feel under pressure is decidedly personal, however, there *are* common issues that affect us all.

Universal stressors are external factors that influence our lives and how much pressure we put ourselves under. The recession, societal expectation, popular culture and the government all play a role in shaping how we think we measure up. For example, the global economic crisis has changed how we plan for the future while societally, the 'having it all' debate can make us competitive, absorbed by what we think other people have and also what we believe other people think we should have. (No boyfriend? FAIL. Hate your job? FAIL.) That whole 'survival of the fittest' schtick didn't only relate to cave-dwelling folk. We're social creatures and we're genetically programmed to strive for meaning in our lives. If you decide you're not up to the challenge it can have a truly negative effect on your outlook.

Then there are the **personal stressors**. The same event can mean something totally different to two separate people. Hell, the same event can have totally different meanings to the same person depending on when it happens. For instance, picture yourself skipping out of the office on a Friday night heading to the pub for a well-earned gin and tonic after a horrible week. You step outside, take a deep breath of freedom … and then your boss calls you back in. Apparently, there's a problem with the project you've been working on and you have to call your colleague in Canada immediately. You feel stressed and angry as you stomp back to your desk. Alternatively, imagine your boss caught you on a Monday night just as you were heading to the Most Boring Dinner Party of All Time which you'd been dreading for weeks. Brilliant – you now have a perfect excuse to miss the party and even if the business call is a disaster you have an entire week to deal with the fallout.

Positive stress

Don't get us wrong, not all stress is bad. Being put under pressure can drive you to achieve and to strive for success. It's also integral to experiencing a sense of achievement. When you're bored or understimulated you tend to perform worse than you do when you're interested in what you're doing. You're not engaged and so you don't really care how it turns out – or you're so confident you can do it there's no pay-off emotionally for completing it.

Stress can be exciting. When you're about to read a speech to 200 people your body is buzzing, your thoughts are racing and you're poised to act. Often humans perform their best when feeling keyed up.

Pressure and performance

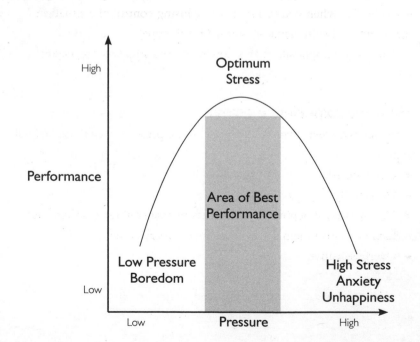

You'll step onto that stage totally alert   and you'll probably perform better because of it. The sense of achievement you'll feel when it's over will be in proportion to how hard you worked on it and the amount of pressure you felt under.

We've been built to survive. As tension rises we're increasingly able to confront stress. Our hearts pump more blood around our bodies, we become more energised and alert and we're ready to face whatever we have to. However, this feeling can reach a peak. It's like a faulty boiler. The whole thing is ticking along merrily until the pressure starts building and building, pipes crack and eventually the whole thing explodes. It's when you feel as if you're losing control of a situation that you start feeling anxious and unable to cope.

The diagram opposite shows how pressure and performance are related.

How we experience stress

Everyone who feels they can't cope with the pressure they're under will appear:

+ Preoccupied
+ Distressed
+ Insular (they'll begin to avoid situations that could stress them out further or give them something else to worry about)
+ Overly sensitive

Example: Lucy's loan

Lucy has just found out that she owes an additional £500 on a loan and has to pay it off immediately or incur lots of interest. She hasn't budgeted for it and hasn't got the money. She's going to have to borrow it from her parents, which makes her feel terrible for a few reasons:

1 She's twenty-eight and feels she shouldn't be asking her parents for money any more.
2 They're retired and are living off their pensions. They need all the money they have.
3 She didn't tell them she'd taken out a loan in the first place so when she calls she'll be delivering a double-dose of bad news.

This stress has made her absent-minded at work – she missed an important meeting and will now have to ask her boss to clarify things again. She also snapped at a co-worker who asked her to do something for the second time. Her heart is beating and her head thumping. She can't help thinking this could intrinsically damage her relationship with her parents.

We're going to put Lucy's experience in a snazzy diagram called a mind map. You'll find we use these throughout the book as a way of illustrating how your thoughts, behaviour, physical health and mood are all linked.

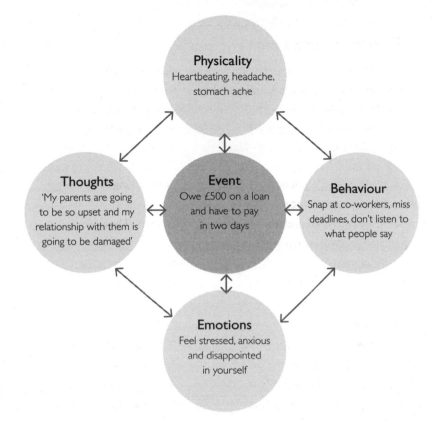

The symptoms of stress

On page 20 we've listed some of the most common symptoms of stress. You'll probably recognise a fair few of them, but others might be a bit more surprising. You might not have associated that particular mood or physical feeling with stress before. If you get angry a lot, you might think it's because you're just 'made that way', rather than a result of stress, for example. People often classify themselves as 'a worrier' or 'a pessimist', without looking for reasons behind this perpetual state of mind.

The list may appear a smidgen intimidating, but it should actually be reassuring. How you're feeling and behaving and reacting to stress is completely normal. Everyone – *everyone* – goes through it and while individual responses vary, they're all along the same lines. People can get hyper and try to do everything at once. They'll drink more, socialise all the time and even talk faster. Alternatively, many people do totally the opposite when stressed. They'll become withdrawn and quiet. They'll question themselves and their decisions. They'll constantly seek reassurance and start isolating themselves from friends and family because they want to avoid any situations that might provoke more stress. Also, experiencing any or all of these symptoms can make falling asleep near enough impossible. Lack of sleep on top of everything else can make you feel, well, completely crazy. And all of that will leave you exhausted, making it even harder to deal with whatever caused the stress in the first place.

People are different, but whatever symptoms you're experiencing please be reassured they're completely and utterly normal.

Ⓢ Symptom checklist

Tick off the symptoms below that apply to you. Starting to think about your personal response to stress will prompt you to consider what is actually causing you to feel this way and how all your reactions are related. This is a good starting point for later strategies that really examine your stress triggers.

Moods/emotions

❑ Anxious
❑ Frustrated
❑ Angry
❑ Sensitive
❑ Defensive

❑ Irritable
❑ Depressed
❑ Fearful
❑ Ashamed
❑ Insecure

❑ Panicky
❑ Out of control
❑ Guilty

Behaviour

❑ Increased drinking/smoking/
drug taking
❑ Over or under eating
❑ Procrastinating
❑ Nail biting
❑ Snapping at people
❑ Poor time management
❑ Distracted/not concentrating
❑ Stopping pleasurable
activities/not looking after
yourself
❑ Difficulty making decisions
❑ Prone to accidents/becoming
clumsy

❑ Becoming a workaholic
❑ Absenteeism/withdrawing
(both professionally and
socially)
❑ Becoming reckless
❑ Hyper/always in a rush
❑ Talk more/faster
❑ Forgetful (e.g. forget
your keys/to lock up/
call someone/leave your
wallet at home)
❑ Constantly seek
reassurance

Thoughts

- ❏ Worried and negative
- ❏ Self-focused (the whole world's out to get me/why does this always happen to me?)
- ❏ Blaming yourself (this is my fault/I always mess things up)
- ❏ Comparative (she wouldn't have messed this up)
- ❏ Fearing the worst
- ❏ Doubting your ability to cope
- ❏ Taking things personally
- ❏ Vague
- ❏ Ruminating (dwelling on things and going over and over them)
- ❏ Unstructured

Physicality

- ❏ Tension in neck and shoulders – general aches and pains
- ❏ Muscular cramps and spasms
- ❏ Nervous twitches
- ❏ Chest pains
- ❏ Increased heart rate
- ❏ Constipation or diarrhoea
- ❏ Dizziness
- ❏ Pins and needles
- ❏ Difficulty swallowing
- ❏ Feeling sluggish or feeling restless
- ❏ Insomnia
- ❏ Loss of concentration
- ❏ Increased or decreased appetite
- ❏ Sweating
- ❏ Breathlessness
- ❏ Exhaustion
- ❏ Spot outbreaks/skin irritations
- ❏ Loss of libido
- ❏ Tendency to contract colds, infections

Why do we feel stressed?

Stress is commonly divided into two categories: acute and chronic.

Acute stress is the most common form and is provoked by 'short-term' stressors. It comes from recent demands put upon you, both in the recent past and near future. This is the kind of stress we mentioned above that can be very positive. It can drive you to succeed and actually make you feel great – for example a job interview can lead to acute stress, but when you're done you can feel exhilarated and proud of yourself. As can your upcoming wedding: there's so much to organise and the big day's looming, but it's exciting. Timescale is an important factor here. Acute stresses are caused by things you're dealing with now or that will happen in the near future – either way there is an end in sight. If your car was involved in a crash, the business of fixing it and of being car-less for a few weeks will be stressful, but when your car is fixed it'll stop. The same goes for losing your phone, having to chair a meeting, having to see your ex at a dinner party, losing an important document, etc. All these things can be exceptionally stressful while they last.

The issue of control is also important: acute stressors are normally things that you do have some influence over (i.e. you can get your car fixed, prepare for the meeting or avoid your ex). Because of this – and because there's normally a time limit on them – they tend to have less long-term impact than chronic stressors.

Chronic stress is long-term pressure caused by things that don't have a definitive end date and over which you don't have much, if any, control. For example: being in an unhappy marriage; having a job you hate, but needing the money; having a dysfunctional family; a physical health problem or being in debt. This kind of stress can be utterly debilitating and lead to anxiety and depression. If you are living with a constant source of angst it can chip away at your self-esteem and make you question yourself and your decision-making capabilities. You can feel permanently exhausted and rundown. Everything becomes harder to deal with – the stress spirals to include lots of other stuff (e.g. you're withdrawn so haven't seen your friends; you now worry what they think of you and whether you've upset them) so the original stressor isn't even at the forefront of your mind any more. It's just always in the background like permanent white noise.

Chronic stress is very dangerous because it can become so internalised people forget it's even there – it becomes so much a part of life that you think feeling constantly uptight is totally normal.

Both acute and chronic stress aren't only caused by bad things happening – they can also be caused by good things not happening. For example, the job interview you were so excited about: if it goes horribly wrong and you don't get the job it can cause you lots of stress. You might start questioning what you're going to do now, or how you'll tell your friends and family, etc.

Disappointment and the fear of disappointment also play a big role. You might be so frightened that something may not live up to your expectations that you put unnecessary pressure on yourself and push yourself beyond your capabilities – or alternatively not push yourself at all, in which case you'll feel stressed because you're setting yourself up for a fall. You might even sabotage things to ensure they fail so at least you'll feel in control when they do.

These ways of thinking are all based upon external or internal demands.

External and internal demands

External demands: These come from work, family, deadlines, friends, money issues, laws, rules and regulations. The list goes on and on. It's all stuff that is put upon you and not that you put on yourself.

Internal demands: This is the pressure that you put on yourself – your own personal definition of what is acceptable and unacceptable. For example: you have an upcoming test and the result doesn't matter at all as far as your grade is concerned – you've already passed the course with flying colours – but a good result matters to you. Your own personal rules dictate you have to pass. You will therefore put yourself under intense pressure and feel stressed when, externally, there's no pressure at all. It is internal demands that lead to self-criticism, self-judgement and the setting of intimidatingly high standards.

How and why you get stressed is therefore not just down to the specific event or situation that you find yourself in, it's also down to your own internal judgements, ideas, hopes and values.

While you might not be able to change the stressor itself you can change how you deal with it, which will have a huge impact on your life and general well-being.

Nature versus nurture

Ah, the classic debate: how much of who you are is down to your genetics and how much is down to your upbringing? Well, when it comes to stress they both play a part.

Nature: Your temperament makes you who you are. Whatever face you show publicly, internally you are built to respond to things a certain way. Some people are more sensitive than others and therefore are naturally more prone to stress. Your body's arousal response (fight or flight) is triggered more quickly and takes longer to calm down.

Nurture: Our experience of the world as a kid shapes our belief system as an adult. What you learned as a child – whether positive or negative – will have influenced how you see things and experience things now. For example, if your parents were incredibly cautious it's likely you were taught to view certain things as threatening and so be more predisposed to feel stress. Also, if your parents weren't good at dealing with pressure themselves it's unlikely they'd have passed on effective and lasting coping mechanisms. However, if your family were carefree and embraced new things, you'll have grown up feeling more confident about facing pressure head-on.

Our ability to cope with stress improves with experience (like pretty much everything). If you've done your best to avoid new challenges for fear of not succeeding or not being able to cope when something genuinely worrying does happen that you can't ignore or avoid you'll be far less likely to be able to handle it. Of course there are exceptions to every rule, but whatever belief system you've grown up with – or inherited – it'll have a big impact on how you view and handle stressful events.

Next steps …

In this book we will teach you strategies and techniques to deal with stress. Recognising how and why you might behave, think and feel the way you do is the first step in learning how to change these patterns of behaviour and to feeling calmer.

Thoughts to take away

✓ You can change how you react to stress and increase confidence in your ability to cope

✓ Learning to manage both short-term and long-term stress will make you feel more in control

✓ Stop putting yourself under unnecessary pressure – remember, there's no such thing as perfect

2

Cognitive Behavioural Therapy

We explain what Cognitive Behavioural Therapy is all about and how you can start using it to beat stress, worry and anxiety.

What is CBT?

If this is the first time you've ever heard of Cognitive Behavioural Therapy (CBT), we appreciate that it might sound like some kind of assessment process from science-fiction novels. Thankfully that couldn't be further from the truth. It is one of the leading evidence-based treatments for dealing with mental health issues. And yes – stress, anxiety and worry can be classed as mental health issues.

Times are changing and thankfully mental health isn't the taboo subject it once was. Due to high-profile campaigns by charities (such as MIND and Time to Change), information groups and even celebrities, people don't necessarily run for the hills when you mention mental well-being any more. This is obviously wonderful, but unfortunately there is still a stigma attached to admitting you're not coping with something. You can feel that you're somehow letting everyone down by not being able to just 'pull yourself together'. This is total rubbish. Stress and anxiety can become crippling problems once they've got their claws into you and they can massively affect your life. 'Get over it' is not brilliant advice, trust us. You're absolutely not a failure for feeling like you do. It's completely normal. Taking steps to learn how to cope with it is the best thing you could ever do. Which is where CBT comes in.

Pioneered by Dr Aaron T. Beck in the 1960s, CBT is now recommended by the National Institute of Clinical Excellence (NICE) as a highly effective treatment for a wide variety of disorders from depression and anxiety to insomnia and Obsessive Compulsive Disorder (OCD). It's focused on finding practical strategies to manage the problems you face. And once you've practised the techniques you'll have them for life so you can fall back on them whenever you need them.

We believe how you interpret a situation affects your mood, your behaviour, your physicality and your thoughts. This is the fundamental basis of CBT.

In the simplest possible terms, the way you perceive an event will influence what you're going to think, do and how you're going to feel both emotionally and physically. You actively construct the meaning of what goes on around you and then act on it.

Example: Rebecca's rage

Rebecca and her boyfriend, Jack, were in the process of buying a flat together which was A Really Big Deal. Not only had they managed to scrape enough money together for a deposit, but it represented a gigantic step forward in their relationship.

They were so close to getting the keys – all they had to do was sign the contracts and transfer the deposit. They both excitedly scrawled their names across all the paperwork and then Jack took it with him to post on his way to work. He'd absolutely insisted on doing this himself. He and Rebecca constantly argued over his supposed laziness and she thought he wanted to prove to her that he could sort stuff out when it mattered. She was proud of him and pleased he cared. ⋯⋮⋅

⋯∴ A couple of days went by and the lawyer still hadn't received the papers. He informed them that if he hadn't got them by Monday the whole sale would fall through. Panicking, Rebecca asked James why they hadn't arrived and if she could see the receipt from the post office. Jack sheepishly admitted that he hadn't actually posted them himself. He'd given them to an office intern to sort out. He had absolutely no idea where they were or when they were going to arrive. He had sent all of their most personal financial details into Never-Never Land.

Rebecca was apoplectic with rage.

He'd clearly done this on purpose trying to prove that being laid-back was the better way to be and it had backfired. Now they would lose the flat and it would be all his fault!

She screamed at him and went straight to the pub with a friend, ranting all the way. That weekend they barely spoke to each other and Rebecca was torn up by anxiety over what might happen.

First thing Monday morning the lawyer emailed to let them know he'd received the envelope and everything was fine – they'd got the flat. When they picked up the keys their celebration felt tainted and a bit sad.

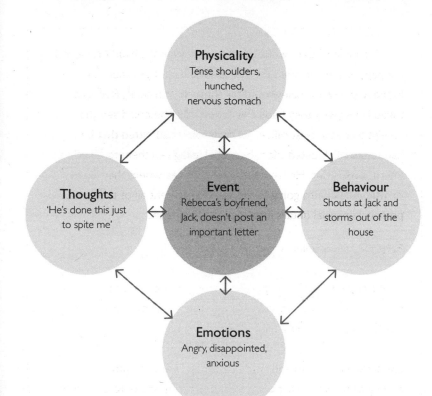

This is Rebecca's mind map. If Rebecca had been calmer she would have interpreted the event differently, leading to a better outcome. She could have let Jack explain himself and they could have worked a way around the problem together (perhaps signing everything in person if the lawyer didn't receive the papers). They wouldn't have spent the whole weekend feeling isolated and anxious, but could have shared their concerns. Rebecca would also have been able to step back and acknowledge that if Jack always cuts corners then clearly he hadn't done this to wind her up, he was just behaving as he normally did.

CBT will teach you how to start really taking note of what you do, how you feel both emotionally and physically and to start questioning your thoughts and their validity. Gradually you'll be able to change a stress-inducing gut reaction to a calmer and more measured one.

How to understand stress using CBT

CBT is all about recognising that it's not actually the stressor that makes you stressed, but the way you interpret it. Take Rebecca. The fact that Jack hadn't posted the letters the way she would have done caused her stress on so many levels because she interpreted the situation as a personal affront and as a precursor for disaster. If she'd interpreted it as just an annoyance she would have saved herself a lot of hair pulling.

The psychologist Arnold Allan Lazarus reckons that there are two separate stages of interpretation that the human mind goes through when confronted with a stressful situation:

Primary appraisal: Is there a problem?
Secondary appraisal: Can I cope with the problem?

Stressful event $\longrightarrow$ Primary appraisal $\longrightarrow$ Secondary appraisal $\longrightarrow$

> Physical response
> Emotional response
> Behavioural response

When it comes to stress it's not just about how big the problem is, it's also about whether you think you can cope or not. This is affected by how many external and internal demands there are on you, how in control you feel, the length of time the event's been going on for (or will go on for) and also the sort of person you are. For instance, say you were on an awful team building weekend away and there was a power cut in the hotel. Everyone was gathered together in the hotel restaurant to wait it out. Your primary assessment might be, 'This is a disaster. Now I'm stuck in a crap hotel with a bunch of colleagues and I can't even hide away in my room.' However, Clare, who is also on the trip, could think, 'Well, at least we'll all have something to talk about now.' Primary appraisals differ from person to person. Where one person sees a problem, another might see an opportunity.

Primary appraisals decide whether you interpret an event as a definitive problem which will result in anxiety and low mood, or as an obstacle to be overcome resulting in growth and development. Challenging events can therefore be destructive (where you see problems as bigger than you) or constructive (things to be tackled head-on).

Next are the secondary appraisals. You've already decided the power cut is a problem – now you need to work out whether you can cope. If your next thought is, 'The tills aren't working so I can't even buy a drink at the bar – this is the worst night of my life,' your stress levels are going to skyrocket. Whereas, Clare, who's already decided the power cut isn't a problem, will think, 'At least the manager is quite funny and they're giving out free food.'

Even in situations that everyone would consider stressful (e.g. a power cut) people's secondary appraisals will be totally different. If you find your strengths and abilities lacking (for example your ability to make conversation with your colleagues or to enjoy their company) you'll be distressed and feel like giving up. Anxiety will begin to eat you up, colouring everything else and you'll start seeing everything negatively. You'll screen out any potential good news to fit your negative view: 'Ugh. This complimentary sandwich is disgusting.'

Opposite we've drawn out a mind map and on page 38 a vicious circle showing what's going on in your head when you're thinking this negatively. The mind map shows how a negative primary and secondary appraisal will affect your behaviour, physicality and emotions, while the vicious circle shows how thinking, acting and feeling you can't cope just breeds more insecurity so you actually start worrying about your worry.

While primary and secondary appraisals suggest your thought processes are the most important factors in how you assess your stress levels, this isn't always true. For instance, someone might get bad news and instantly punch a wall (behaviour), which will make their hand hurt and their heart race (physical response), leading to negative thoughts ('Now I've screwed up my hand and the wall, and I have to deal with the original problem.'), and their mood will not only be stressed, but probably angry and frustrated too.

Whatever your first response, CBT will change your gut-reaction primary and secondary appraisals so you'll automatically try to see the solutions to problems rather than dwelling on the negatives.

The thought, physicality and behavioural stages can all act as intervention points. At the moment your default settings for these

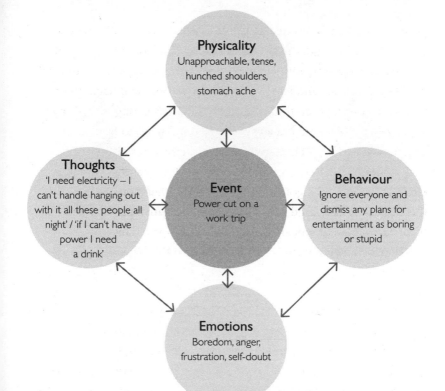

stages are programmed negatively. However, if you change just one of them to be more positive, this will have a knock-on effect on the others which will in turn influence your mood.

How CBT works and how it will help you

CBT aims to help you to:

+ Identify the sources of stress

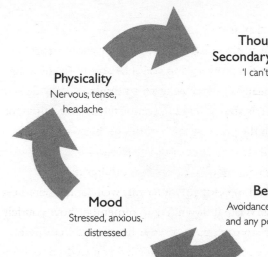

**Thoughts /
Secondary appraisal**
'I can't cope.'

Physicality
Nervous, tense,
headache

Behaviour
Avoidance of the problem
and any potential solutions

Mood
Stressed, anxious,
distressed

+ Change your primary and secondary appraisals of the event
+ Look at what you're doing that might be contributing to the problem
+ Learn strategies and techniques to help you manage and reduce stress
+ Re-assess counter-productive beliefs and interpretations
+ Test out alternative interpretations
+ Restructure your priorities

CBT is an active approach to solving problems. While reading about it is all well and good, you're going to have to try out the exercises if you want to see proper permanent changes.

⑤ Your own mind map

We'd like you to fill in a mind map. Thinking deeply about a specific event will break down the problem and you'll be able to see how stress is affecting you personally. You may believe that thinking 'Why does this always happen to me?' is an off-the-cuff, completely justified thought that means nothing in the grand scheme of things, but you'd be wrong. That one thought is likely to change your behaviour, affect your physical well-being and cause your mood to drop. These things matter.

To fill out your mind map identify a recent, well-remembered event that caused you stress. Write it down. Try to remember how you felt physically – did your stomach drop or your heart race? Recall what worries went through your mind, what this led you to do or want to do (behaviour) and how you felt emotionally. Flick back to our list of the common emotions that are symptomatic of stress in Chapter 1 to jog your memory if needed.

We have filled out an example on page 40 to help you get started.

Completing a mind map will have given you an insight into how you personally deal with stress. Note down which part you found it easiest to fill out. You might, for example, experience physical reactions very strongly and work from there, i.e. you remember suddenly tensing up and getting a feeling in your stomach like you were on a rollercoaster. From there you recall that those symptoms were caused by the thought, 'I'm going to ruin the wedding,' etc. Whatever you remembered first is your starting point and from there you can fill in the gaps. The better you get at identifying all four parts of the map the more options you'll give yourself later on for making changes and feeling calmer.

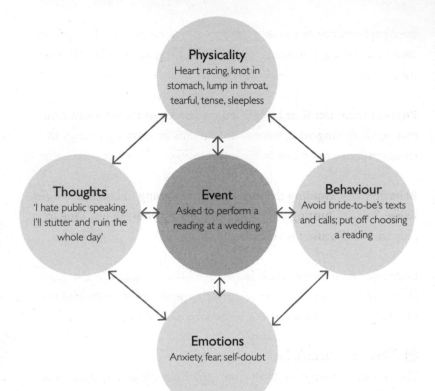

Soon you'll be able to challenge your thoughts, your physical response and your behaviour, which will then influence your mood. Using the example above we've suggested the kind of challenges you should start thinking about below.

Thoughts: If you did stutter during the reading, would it really ruin the entire wedding? No one else will be paying as much attention to your performance as you. Also, everyone will be in a good mood. You could do nothing but sneeze up there and everyone would still make the best of it.

Physical response: Your body is letting you know there's a situation that needs dealing with. You can control this by learning relaxation techniques (more on this in the next chapter).

Behaviour: By avoiding the problem it's just going to continue or get worse. You risk hurting your friend and giving yourself less time to prepare and practise the reading.

Challenging any one of these points would have a domino effect, changing the others and ultimately lifting your mood so your new mind map would look something like the one on page 42.

Ⓢ Thoughts aren't facts

This is a key message we'll be advocating throughout the book. When you think, 'I can't do this'/ 'They all hate me' / 'I'm not good enough', it's very easy just to accept these thoughts as facts and feel terrible about them. They are just thoughts, not facts. They're hypotheses coming from your negatively biased brain, representations of how you feel about yourself at that particular moment which, more often than not, have no basis in reality.

We want you to become more aware of this so whenever you catch yourself thinking something bad about yourself as if it's a fundamental truth, you can challenge and change it. For example, 'I can't do

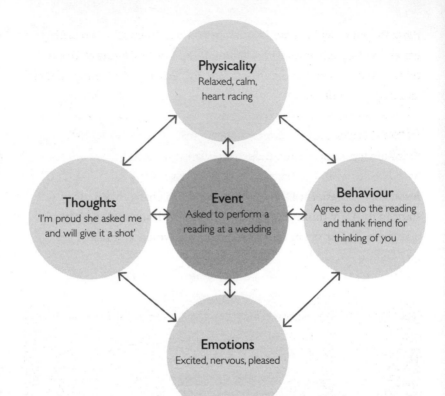

this' should become 'I think I can't do this'. It's a small, but hugely important difference that will encourage you not to simply accept this kind of thinking as factual without any proof. Okay, you think you can't do this … but is that really the case? What abilities and skills do you have that might enable you to do it? Have you ever managed to do something similar before? Try to find alternative views to discredit it and be fair on yourself when you think it through. Confronting these thoughts will flag up how often you put yourself down with generalised all-encompassing statements and instead prompt you to think, 'Well, maybe I could do this or this', leaving you feeling calmer and more in control.

Next steps ...

Practice filling out a mind map using various stressful scenarios that have affected you. The better you get at identifying your different responses the easier it'll be when you want to change them. By starting to really think about how you deal with stress you're already questioning your default negative settings – which will make you feel calmer.

Thoughts to take away

✓ CBT *will* change your instinctual responses to stress, making you feel more in control

✓ The way you think, behave and feel physically and emotionally are all interlinked – if you change one for the better the rest will follow

✓ How stressed you feel totally depends on your interpretation of an event. Altering and questioning your immediate appraisals will make you calmer

Take a Deep Breath

The physical effects of stress are often the most noticeable and the most debilitating. We'll explain why stress affects you in this way and what you can do to calm your body down.

Wearing your stress on your sleeve

When you say you 'feel stressed' it's more than likely you mean you're experiencing it both mentally and physically. Your mind is whirring and your body is riled up. The more negative and panicky your thoughts, the more overt your body's response will be. This can be exceptionally draining. Not only are you worrying about the original issue, but you're also having to concern yourself with uncomfortable physical reactions and worry about whether they're noticeable to anyone else.

Humans interact through physical representations of their emotions and thoughts (also known as non-verbal cues). For example, when you feel pleased you'll smile, when you feel angry you'll scowl and when you feel scared you'll tremble. There are, of course, dozens of nuances that you transmit, but your appearance and how you portray yourself physically is often the first and truest indication people have of what you're really thinking and how you really feel.

People understand what most physical responses represent, mainly because the majority of them are pretty damn obvious – including our response to stress. Blurred vision, breathlessness, trembling, a nervous stomach and dizziness are all pretty hard to hide and experiencing them isn't exactly pleasant. You'll probably look disorientated, confused or preoccupied. Your back will be hunched, you'll be fidgeting and possibly shaking and visibly sweating. These physical symptoms can be extremely debilitating and severely affect your day-to-day life.

The fight or flight response

No matter how many technological gadgets you own or swanky

clothes you wear, there's no getting away from the fact that
fundamentally we're animals. We still have the same ingrained survival
instincts that our cavemen and cavewomen ancestors relied upon so
heavily and just because we don't have to club sabre-toothed tigers on
the head to survive any more doesn't mean these primitive instincts
have disappeared.

We have an automatic inborn reaction to stress and anxiety called
the 'fight or flight response' triggered by a perception of threat or
danger. Imagine you're doing some gardening when suddenly a
massive tiger jumps out of the bushes in front of you, pawing the
ground and flashing its not so tiny teeth. You have two choices: either
fight the tiger or start sprinting in the opposite direction. Both of
these options will require excessive physical strength and to facilitate
this, your sympathetic (and very efficient) nervous system floods your
body with adrenaline and cortisol. Your heart starts beating faster,
pumping blood away from the places that don't need it to the muscles
and limbs that now need additional fuel. These muscles will tense up
ready for action. Your respiratory rate increases, forcing more oxygen
into your bloodstream and heightening your senses: your pupils dilate
to sharpen your sight, your ears turn into pin-sharp microphones
and your perception of pain diminishes. Blood is also diverted away
from the skin's surface and your fingers and toes, which can result in
paleness, tingling and 'cold feet'. This is so if the tiger catches a swipe
of you you're less likely to bleed to death (disgusting, but very clever).
You also begin to sweat to keep from overheating.

You are in 'attack mode', prepared, both physically and
psychologically, for either fight or flight. Your rational mind has taken a

backseat – when faced with a tiger you don't have time to think, 'Why the hell is there a tiger in my garden?', it's there so you have to deal with it. Your body knows thoughts like this will only slow you down so it doesn't give them a look in. When you feel this way everything is a potential threat. You'll overreact to the slightest provocation as your sense of fear is as at survival pitch.

Then, when you've dodged the tiger, locked yourself in the shed and called the local zoo, your parasympathetic system kicks in: your nerves release noradrenaline which help to reverse the changes that have taken place, gradually cooling you down and returning everything to normal.

Isn't that whole process amazing? Well, kind of.

Fight or flight used to be integral for human survival. The trouble is, thousands and thousands of years later we're still programmed exactly the same. Our fight or flight system is just as sensitive as it ever was and is triggered whenever we feel fear, anxiety or stress. Now that we're not stumbling over sabre-toothed tigers on a daily basis feeling this way can be very inconvenient. Money problems, relationship troubles, health concerns and horrendous bosses can't be bested by fighting or running away (except perhaps the boss). However, your body doesn't know that and prepares you just the same. Adrenaline and cortisol are quick to kick in and all rational thoughts fly out of the window. Noradrenaline is slow to calm you down, meaning physically it can take ages to feel normal again.

And that's not all. Fight or flight doesn't only happen with real tangible problems (i.e. tigers, money issues or losing your job), but also imagined ones, for instance fearing you've embarrassed yourself or being scared of criticism. In our current high-pressure, high-

demand culture, the body's stress response is activated so often that
sometimes it doesn't have a chance to return to normal, resulting in a
state of on-going tension.

When you suffer from recurring stress your body and mind lose
their ability to deal with day-to-day realities. The physical change
you've gone through is dramatic. The fact that blood has been
diverted away from the bits that don't need it can result in nausea or
constipation as your digestive tract shuts down. Your glands will stop
secreting saliva, resulting in a dry mouth, while your rapid breathing
can cause dizziness and hot flushes. All of these things will make it
harder to sleep, leading to exhaustion. It's perhaps not surprising then
that experiencing these conditions regularly can eventually leave you
feeling sapped of all energy physically and mentally.

The physical chill-out

Relaxation should be a simple and foolproof way to rid yourself of
tension. Loads of people think they know how to relax, but in reality
have no idea. Lying in a bath and staring at the ceiling thinking about
all the things you should be doing isn't relaxing. There's a skill to
relaxation and it takes practice. If you're someone who experiences
stress regularly then it's pretty likely you need to learn how to relax
and invest as much time unwinding as you do in the things that make
you feel anxious.

It's physically impossible to feel both relaxed and stressed at the
same time – like sneezing with your eyes open – so learning how to
chill out is an essential skill for everyone.

And relax …

Decide when and where you're going to relax so that it is planned in advance. Book some time into your diary (you're far more likely to stick to it if you've actually 'booked it in').

There are three techniques to try: muscle relaxation, breathing exercises, and visualisation techniques. Please try all of them at least a couple of times and really go for it. One will, no doubt, appeal to you more than the others, but it's important to give all of them a shot because you might be surprised by which one helps you and which one you're good at. Once you've found the technique you're most comfortable with, schedule it into your week or better yet, do it whenever and wherever you need to. Even if you're at work you should be able to find a quiet place to get ten minutes to yourself.

And – the most important bit – don't judge yourself. Even if you're the most cynical person in the world, just give it a go. Don't blame yourself or get frustrated if you don't think it's working the first few times – these things take practice. Just trying to relax is better than not relaxing at all. Once you're better at it whenever you notice your body is tense you'll be able to stop your fight or flight response kicking in or calm down more quickly when it has.

Ⓢ Progressive muscle relaxation

When stressed your muscles are naturally in a state of tension, but because your mind is on other things you might not notice this for some time. Tensing and releasing various muscle groups throughout the body produces a state of deep relaxation and will clear your mind because you're concentrating on your body rather than on everyday

Talking to motivate and focus yourself

Throughout this exercise we'll be asking you to talk to yourself at certain points, either out loud or in your head. This is really important. It means you are consciously taking control of the exercise – rather than just tensing your muscles, you are choosing to. You are also taking your mind off your stress. There's no point tensing your leg and then continuing to think about what's stressing you out. By talking yourself through it you are forcing your mind to focus on your body, giving it some much needed distance from outside concerns.

troubles. When you next tense up your body will recognise the feeling immediately (because of an ingrained muscle memory) and will know how to calm down. If worrying thoughts do scuttle back into your head, kick them out and re-focus on the task at hand.

If you tense a muscle for a few seconds and then release it the muscle will relax completely – much more than it would if you hadn't tensed it.

To start
+ Sit down. Go as limp as you can from head to foot
+ Put your shoulders back and let your shoulder blades go slightly flat
+ Wriggle your feet and stretch out your legs
+ Shake your arms gently, rolling the backs of your hands against the floor or your thighs

✦ Look from side to side, gently rolling your head forward so you're looking at your lap

Legs

✦ Raise one leg six to ten inches above the floor

✦ Point your toes towards the ceiling. Hold this position of tension for ten seconds or until you begin to feel the muscles tremble, then say to yourself, 'Let go'. At this point stop pointing and let the leg drop back to the floor. Rest for another ten seconds, saying, 'I feel the tension flowing out of my leg ... my leg feels warm, heavy ... and completely relaxed'

✦ Repeat this once more with the same leg before starting again with the other

Bum and thighs

✦ Tighten your bum and thigh muscles at the same time. Hold for as long as you can until you have to release them, saying 'Let go' to yourself. Pause for ten seconds, really focusing on how good the muscles feel now they're relaxed

✦ Repeat

Stomach

✦ Practice exactly the same procedure on your abdominal muscles

✦ Repeat

Back and neck

✦ Think about tightening all the muscles along your spine. Arch your back, stretching it from your tailbone to your neck. Hold it and then relax by telling yourself to let go

✦ Repeat

Arms and shoulders

+ Imagine there is a bar suspended above your head that you're using to pull yourself up. Clench your fists around it as hard as you can. Flex the muscles in your arms and shoulders, hunch your shoulders tightly, hold for as long as possible and then say, 'Let go.' Relax for ten seconds, soaking up the warm, relaxed feelings and letting the tension flow out

+ Repeat

Jaw

+ Tighten your jaw muscles, clamping down on you back teeth as if you're about to grind them. Hold for as long as you can and then say, 'Let go' and relax

+ Repeat

Face

+ Screw up your facial muscles into a grimace – as if you're entering a gurning competition. Hold for at least ten seconds until you can really feel the tension across your face. Say, 'Let go' and relax

+ Repeat

Eyes

+ Lean back and focus on a point on the ceiling. Without moving your head, slowly roll your eyes as far as they will go to the right, then to the centre, then to the left, then back to the centre

+ Rub the palms of your hands together until you feel heat. Close your eyes and cover them with your hands. Let the heat warm them. Say, 'Let go', remove your hands and relax

Entire body

+ Clench your feet and fists. Pull your shoulders up. Tighten your jaw and face. Now flex your entire body, arching your back as far as you can from your heels to the back of your head. Hold it for as long as you can until you feel your body tremble. Then say, 'Let go' and completely relax, feeling the tension drain away

And finally

+ Close your eyes. Let your attention wander slowly over each part of your body, from legs to face. If any area seems to have some residual tension, tense it even further. Then let go and picture the tension leaving your body like liquid draining from a glass

+ Stay in this state for a couple of minutes. Keep thinking about your body, focusing on your muscles and how rested they feel. If your thoughts turn to potentially stressful things, don't scold yourself, just bring them gently back to your body. Tell yourself, 'I am relaxed now. My legs feel relaxed. My bum, thighs, and abdomen feel relaxed. My back arms, shoulders, jaws, face and eyes feel relaxed. The tension has gone'

⑤ Deep breathing

When you're stressed you'll often start breathing faster as your body prepares itself for fight or flight or alternatively you'll hold your breath. Focusing on your breathing physically forces your body to calm down, which will give you more breathing space in your head too. Best of all, it doesn't take long and you can do it anywhere.

+ Place one hand on your chest and one hand on your abdomen

+ Breath slowly (preferably through your nose with your mouth shut)

+ As you inhale push your abdomen out against your hand – feel your abdomen expand and your hand rise

+ Hold for two seconds

+ Exhale slowly through your nose – feel your stomach deflate and your hand fall

+ Smile as you exhale. (Smiling actually makes you feel happier.) Picture someone you love or a place that makes you feel good – anything that will inspire a smile

⑤ Escape routes

We're now going to suggest something a little bit out there, but bear with us. The idea is this: create a beautifully relaxing place in your mind … then go there and really experience it. Every taste, smell, sound and sight should become embedded in your head. If you truly believe you're in this place it will become your escape. You can shape it into a memory and transport yourself there whenever you're feeling stressed, getting an injection of positivity no matter what's going on.

To start

+ Go somewhere quiet and peaceful where you won't be disturbed

+ Lie down or sit somewhere comfortable

+ Take several long, deep breaths (using the deep-breathing exercise). Picture your stressful thoughts being expelled with each breath

+ Scan your body, taking note of any areas of tension and then let it all out (using the progressive muscle relaxation exercise on pages 50–4 if you need to)

This is just a sample escape route. You can use this one or think of your own – any place that makes you feel calm and stress-free. Imagine it

Example: Escape route

Picture yourself walking through a wide-open field. It's warm, the sun is shining and the sky is a perfect blue. You stroll across it and see a river. You walk towards it. It's shaded by beautiful trees which cast a dappled light over the scene. You reach the edge and sit down, taking off your shoes and dipping your toes in the cool water. You lie down and take a deep breath of the clear, crisp air. Your fingers splay over smooth pebbles at your side. You can hear the water running past you and feel the cool refreshing waves sweeping around your feet. Soft white clouds make shapes in the sky above your head. You can smell the soil underneath you, the long grass and the scent of woodland. You have never felt so relaxed and at peace.

You take a long deep breath and let it slowly out. Rest for as long as you like. And then, when you're ready, gently bring your attention back to the room.

in full colour and surround-sound. What can you see, hear, touch, smell and even taste? If you do really throw yourself into it and try to visualise the scene it can become a wonderfully calming technique for whenever you feel stressed. Just focus your entire mind on bringing back the memory of this place. The more you do it the quicker you'll be able to access your escape route and invoke the feeling of calm.

Next steps ...

A quick failsafe way to immediately feel less stressed physically is to drop your shoulders and push them back. We often don't even notice we're hunching until we feel an ache in our shoulders.

Think about getting yourself a relaxation trigger. Set an alarm on your phone to go off every day that just says 'relax', but make sure the alarm itself isn't alarming (groan) – perhaps a bird call or soft whistle, nothing jarring. Or you could carry a scent that sparks a happy memory or reminds you of your escape route. Anything that will force you to make a concerted effort to relax.

Consider taking up Yoga, Pilates, meditation or Tai Chi. These are brilliant ways to exercise and become more aware of your body. They'll help with many stress-related conditions, including anxiety, headaches, high blood pressure and asthma.

Thoughts to take away

✓ Fight or flight is an automatic primitive response to stress. Learning how to minimise its effects will make you calmer

✓ Making relaxation a priority in your life will permanently change the effect of stress on your body

✓ Altering your physical response to stress will have a calming effect on your thoughts, your behaviour and your mood

4

Attacking Anxiety

Anxiety can chew you up and spit you out … if you let it. Here we explain what anxiety actually is and how and why it's affecting you. As with stress, understanding it is the first step in learning how to handle it.

Anxious about anxiety

Anxiety is one of the most common reactions to stress. Using an example we've mentioned previously, imagine your friend has asked you to perform a reading at her wedding. Public speaking can be stressful for anyone, but particularly at such an emotional event with a lot of expectation surrounding it – not wanting to let your friend down by tripping on the stage and crushing the vicar is totally natural. Those concerns are the result of stress. Anxiety comes in when you really start panicking – when you're actually frightened of the world imploding if you forget your lines.

Anxiety is when normal feelings of pressure and responsibility morph into feelings of fear and vulnerability. It's important to note that within this book we're approaching anxiety as a response to stress rather than as a reaction to an anxiety disorder (such as phobias, Obsessive Compulsive Disorder, health anxiety or generalised anxiety disorder). If you're experiencing any of those, please see your GP for further help.

What is anxiety?

Anxiety is a response to a perceived threat or danger to either your physical or psychological well-being, e.g. when someone leaps out from behind a tree screaming, 'BOO!' (physical), or when you're made redundant (psychological). How anxious you feel (and whether you'll feel anxious at all) is dictated by your situation and what you're doing, how you feel physically, what you're thinking and how you feel emotionally. But, more often than not, it's a combination of all of the above.

When you're anxious the same fight or flight response kicks in that is triggered when you are stressed. Its main aim is to protect and prepare you to either fight or run away from a perceived threat, which is brilliant when that threat is a lunatic cyclist about to mow you down on the street, but not so great when it's a broken boiler that doesn't give a damn how alert your senses are.

However, just like stress, anxiety isn't all bad. It's a totally normal, ingrained human response designed to protect you. On a very basic level, it's alerting you to possible danger so you can work out ways to save yourself. Research has shown that moderate amounts of anxiety can actually increase performance – your body and mind become tuned to the 'threat' so all your energy is focused on it, i.e. you're made redundant and immediately start updating your CV and contacting potential new employers.

Anxiety is an emotion, just like being happy or sad. And, just like happiness and sadness, the feeling should pass as situations change and you move up and down your emotional spectrum. You'll never be able to get rid of anxiety completely – you can't choose never to feel anxious again – but you can manage it differently so you don't get stuck in the feeling. As mentioned above anxiety can be a good thing, but you shouldn't ever be feeling anxious all the time or in reaction to things that don't warrant it (i.e. if the phone rings and you're too nervous to answer it, but have no reason to be).

Anxiety can drastically affect your life, making you behave out of character, think negatively and feel physically and mentally drained. Some typical reactions to anxiety are illustrated in the following mind map over the page.

By limiting your anxiety, you'll be limiting your stress-levels. The

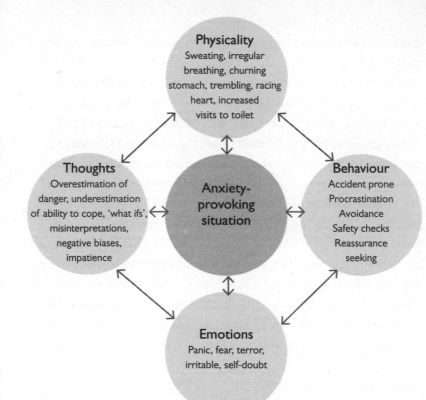

Physicality
Sweating, irregular breathing, churning stomach, trembling, racing heart, increased visits to toilet

Thoughts
Overestimation of danger, underestimation of ability to cope, 'what ifs', misinterpretations, negative biases, impatience

Anxiety-provoking situation

Behaviour
Accident prone
Procrastination
Avoidance
Safety checks
Reassurance seeking

Emotions
Panic, fear, terror, irritable, self-doubt

demands on you won't feel as daunting and you'll be able to deal with all manner of things that previously would have sent you shuffling to bed clutching a flannel to your forehead.

When anxiety becomes a problem

Anxiety is like an annoying reminder – a teeny tiny alarm ringing in the back of your head, alerting you to danger and/or stress: Did I lock the car door? Did I turn my hair straighteners off? Did I pay that bill on time? And it doesn't let future events off the hook either: Will I get another job? Will I have time to write that proposal by Wednesday?

If you find yourself feeling anxious a lot – every day or near enough – it's a problem. It will start to interfere with other aspects of your life that have nothing to do with the original stressor. For example, Sarah knows she won't be able to meet a deadline for a piece of work. Whenever she thinks about it she gets a thrill of fear, which triggers the fight or flight response. Both her breathing and heart go full throttle and she becomes hyper-focused on nothing but her fear. As described in Chapter 3, rational thought will have left the building at this stage, so the email she was in the middle of writing will either lie forgotten or she'll whizz off a curt response that she otherwise would have taken more time over. Now, because she's behaved in a way she normally wouldn't (by sending a curt email) she's also given herself something else to worry about.

Anxiety is problematic when:
+ It's exaggerated and not proportionate to the actual 'danger' of the situation
+ When there's no real danger present at all (you're just imagining it)
+ When it is experienced too frequently (when you over-estimate danger) or too intensely (when you're being overly sensitive)
+ When you become fixated on it and on what you see as your obvious inability to cope
+ When you become anxious about the anxiety itself (when your physical response is something you worry about or dread)

A physical and mental overreaction

Your anxiety reflex might have become so hyper-sensitive that it's triggered all the time, not just when it's needed, like a faulty car alarm that goes off whenever a cat wanders past, not just when someone's trying to break in.

Research shows that people who suffer from anxiety disorders systematically overestimate the danger in certain situations and from their own bodily sensations (i.e. an increased heart rate means a heart attack or a minor mistake at work means they're going to get fired) and also their mental processes ('I'm not dealing with this like I should' or 'I'll never get through this').

Overestimations normally take the form of one (or all) of the below:

1 A distorted estimate on the likelihood of a feared event ('I am definitely going to get fired')
2 A distorted estimate on the severity of an event or the severity of the repercussions ('If I mess up my speech I'll ruin the whole wedding')
3 A distorted estimate of one's (in)ability to cope and the lack of support available ('I'm way out of my depth and no one can help me')

Why anxiety won't just disappear

Annoyingly, anxiety doesn't just pop up, wave and then disappear. It tends to hang around like a persistent wasp at a BBQ. Its propensity to loiter is influenced by the below:

✦ **Avoidance:** Avoiding the issue prevents you from assessing the reality of what's happening and how well you can deal with it. If you never confront your worry, you won't be able to disprove

Situations and thoughts that provoke anxiety

Below are some common anxiety provoking situations or ways of thinking. These things will affect everyone regardless of whether they consider themselves prone to stress or not. How much they affect you is dependent on how well you manage your reactions.

+ Believing you have too much work to do and not enough time to complete it
+ Not believing you're talented enough to do the work even if you did have enough time
+ Fear of performing in public
+ Health fears
+ Waiting for an appointment or interview
+ Expecting to be judged, belittled, rejected, humiliated, embarrassed or put down
+ Feeling insecure and not up to scratch
+ Money worries
+ Fears of intimacy and or commitment
+ Concerns about the consequences of your actions i.e. boss being disappointed, a friend being angry, a partner being upset
+ Feeling like you can't say no and becoming overwhelmed by the responsibility
+ The fear of letting people down
+ Fears about the future

your fears. And, even if what's happening genuinely is beyond your coping capabilities, hiding from it still won't help. The problem will just loom ever larger, like a huge shadow over your shoulder. By facing the issue you're giving yourself options – either to deal with it yourself or to ask for help.

Ⓢ **Don't avoid, always confront the issue (see Chapter 9)**

✦ **How you behave:** Anxiety can make you behave totally out of character. Your mind is so wrapped up in the issue you're not giving anything else your full attention. You might be on edge, angry, frustrated or absent minded. Behaving badly, inconsiderately or rashly can create more issues to feel anxious about. (Avoidance also comes under the banner of 'behaviour', but it is such a big issue it deserves its own section!)

Ⓢ **Think before you speak and act.** Be aware that you're in a heightened state and take time before acting when you feel this way.

✦ **The beliefs you have about an event and its consequences:** Your beliefs can become distorted and warped by fear. Anticipating something bad happening and believing you won't be able to cope if it does, will only make things worse and create a vicious cycle of anxiety which has a knock-on effect, altering your judgement and rationale.

Ⓢ **Question your assumptions and test them:** For example, ask yourself, 'Will it really be the end of the world if I ask my boss for an extension on that project?' Surely she'd rather it was late, but great, than on time and rubbish. (See Chapter 8)

Recognition of
symptoms

Increased symptoms

Worry about
symptoms

Increased anxiety

+ **Thinking about your physical symptoms:** Focusing on your
physical response to a situation can often make symptoms worse
and provoke an entirely separate case of anxiety. Say you're feeling
anxious about an appraisal meeting next week at work. You've been
getting regular stomach cramps and headaches. You begin to worry
they're pretty serious so you start taking pills, but they won't go
away. You become so fixated on the physical pain you don't focus
on the meeting and it turns into a vicious circle (pictured above)

Ⓢ **Stop monitoring your symptoms.** If you're responding to anxiety
physically, remind yourself that your body is behaving totally
normally. What you're experiencing is natural and the symptoms
will ease once your anxiety eases. It maybe uncomfortable but it's
nothing to worry about. You can use the distraction techniques in
Chapter 6 to change focus.

How to calm down your anxious mind and body

Since anxiety is caused by stress, and because stress and anxiety are such personal responses to events, it's important to really narrow down exactly what makes you stressed (and therefore anxious). By taking the time to identify the triggers you'll be better able to manage how you respond to them. Monitoring the times during the day when you experience stress, and the events and people that cause it, means you'll be in a much better position to either cut them out of your life altogether (sadly, not always an option) or learn how to deal with them more effectively.

⑤ The stress schedule

Don't worry, you're not going to have to schedule stressful activities into your week, just monitor them when they happen!

Even if you're suffering from chronic (long-term) stress, it's still important to note down your responses to smaller day-to-day things that might be aggravating this stress or piling more on top, leading to anxiety. Getting rid of these or minimising their effects will make coping with long-term pressures more bearable.

Using the following questions as prompts, record everything that provokes an anxious response in you for one week.

+ What happened?
+ What were you doing at the time?
+ Who were you with?
+ Where were you?
+ How did you feel?
+ What were you thinking?
+ What did you do?
+ How did you feel physically?
+ How stressed did you feel?

	Monday	Tuesday	Wednesday
What happened?	Boss asked me to attend a meeting with HR on Wednesday	I got a final warning for an electricity bill I need to pay	Mum asked me to help her with her shopping
What was I doing at the time?	Working on current project which hasn't been going that well	Finally going through the pile of post I'd been avoiding	Popping over for a quick cup of tea
Who was I with?	No one, but colleague next to me heard	Alone	My mum and dad
Where was I?	Working at my desk	At home	At their house
How did I feel?	Worried, anxious, embarrassed	Anxious, panicky, worried	Anxious, guilty
What was I thinking?	'Something must be seriously wrong. I wonder what the girl next to me thought?'	'How am I going to pay this? What if they cut off the electricity?'	'I don't have time, but I can't say no'
What did I do?	Went and hid in the bathroom	Put it to one side to deal with later	Said yes to them and cancelled a work meeting
How did I feel physically?	Shocked – face flushed, stomach fell into my shoes	Sick, nervous, increased heart rate	Tired, tense
Stress rating (0–10, 0 is none and 10 is loads)	8	9	7

It doesn't matter how small or big the list gets – there could be fifty small stressors that bug you throughout the week or one giant one – what matters is recognising when and how it happens, how you felt when it did and how you then behaved. Also, seeing them written down will prompt you to look at them objectively. You might write 'Having to do the washing when I'm really busy' and laugh, because compared to everything else on the list doing the washing doesn't bother you at all. In fact, it gives you a short break from staring at your computer screen. It's amazing how often we assume things are contributing to our stress without properly considering whether they actually are. If you recognise any of those points you can scrub them off your list giving you one less thing to worry about!

Questions to consider at the end of one week:

✦ What are the common themes to your stress and anxiety? (Is it one big event/lots of little events related to one originator/lots of little unrelated things/are they physical (i.e. a meeting) or psychological (i.e. a bill) or a combination of the two?

✦ List all the triggers and be specific (i.e. out of the twelve stressors you noted down did seven of them have to do with that really annoying woman in accounts?)

✦ Now assess whether there's something you can do about it. Can you limit your contact with the woman in accounts? Can you email her rather than talk to her? Can you delegate that aspect of work to someone else? If not, can you set up a meeting with her to discuss how best to proceed in the future?

✦ How did you experience the stress first? (Did you think, 'I can't handle this', or did your stomach lurch?) Working out your immediate response to stress will help you to identify it in the future so the next time a negative thought whizzes through your head you'll know you can challenge it, or the next time your stomach drops you'll be aware of consequent negative thoughts or behaviour

Any problem you've noted down in the stress schedule can (and will) be remedied by the strategies in this book.

Thoughts to take away

✓ You can't stop anxiety altogether, but you can change how you deal with it

✓ Anxiety is a natural symptom of stress so learning how to manage one will limit the negative effects of the other

✓ The stress schedule will force you to confront stress and anxiety and not to just accept them as natural, permanent features of your day

5

Stress Control

Stress and anxiety are both aggravated and alleviated by how much control you have over a situation and also by the demands you're put under by other people and yourself. Here we look at how you can wrestle back control of your life.

Stress: supply and demand

Control, or a lack thereof, is an integral part of stress. When something stressful happens you'll instinctively make an assessment based upon your primary and secondary appraisals, which are influenced by how much control you feel you have over a situation.

Primary appraisal: Is there a problem? What is being demanded of me?
Secondary appraisal: Can I cope with it?

The demands you're facing are twofold: external (what's actually being asked of you) and internal (what you're asking of yourself and what you believe is expected of you).

How you judge your ability to cope with these demands will be influenced and based on the listed opposite:

Stress as balance or imbalance

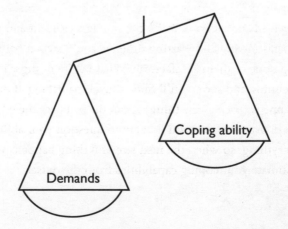

+ The amount of control you feel you have over the situation
+ The skills and tools you have available to you
+ Your experience of similar situations in the past (and whether you succeeded in those situations)
+ Your attitudes and beliefs about stress, anxiety and worry, e.g. whether they're something to be feared or tackled
+ The social support available to you (friends, relatives or a partner)
+ Your physical health
+ Your temperament
+ Knowledge of stress management strategies and your willingness to use them

When day-to-day problems are within your capabilities (when the weighing scales are balanced) you feel in control. However, when you're facing more and more demands – or when one whopping demand comes out of nowhere and smacks you right in the face – your coping abilities can feel stretched to their limit, making you more stressed and anxious. You'll become less efficient and might start procrastinating and wasting time, or you'll switch between tasks finishing none of them satisfactorily. What you're facing will seem overwhelming and soon you'll find yourself panicking. If one more thing happens (even a tiny thing) it can tip you over the edge. This can be a disaster because you'll begin to question your ability to cope with everything, so when the next stressful thing happens you'll underestimate your coping capabilities from the outset.

ⓢ Reduce the demands you're under

Actually getting rid of some stressors is impossible – you can't just magic your teenage son's school exams away (not by any legal means anyway) – but we're willing to bet that there are at least a couple that can be discarded. It's all about prioritising and taking affirmative positive action: ask yourself, 'Do I really need to do that?'

Most demands that can be scrapped will fall into the internal category, things that you expect of yourself or that you believe other people will judge you for. Often this is nonsense, in reality the demand isn't there at all or shouldn't be as stress-inducing as it feels.

You have to reassess what does and doesn't matter – be ruthless with your internal to-do list. If you're someone who always irons their pillowcases but is currently working fourteen-hour days then you need to stop ironing them. If you're someone who always replies via letter to thank people for presents, but you're too busy at the moment, send an email instead. Somewhere along the line all of these things were branded 'essential' according to your personal standards. They're not. Things that won't affect your day-to-day life if you don't do them have to be de-prioritised for your own peace of mind. It's time to be realistic and ignore that voice inside your head telling you you're a disappointment if you let some stuff go – you're absolutely not.

Go through your stress schedule and pick out the issues that you don't actually have to deal with – and then scrap them from your life. Also, add anything that you didn't originally write down because you saw it as essential at the time. Things like ironing your pillowcases can become such integral parts of your routine that you see them as necessary and you don't even recognise them as stresses or time-wasters. Write them into the list so you're acknowledging that they do cause you stress and then erase them from your day-to-day life.

S Increase your coping abilities

Managing the stuff you can't get rid of effectively will make you feel calmer and more in control.

1 Get organised

Decluttering your life will declutter your mind. No matter how much you believe you're untroubled by mess, it will be affecting you and adding to your stress levels. If you're one of those people who reckons they can work brilliantly sitting amongst a pile of debris, congratulations – but there will come a time when you need that bit of paper you last saw under the sofa and stress, anxiety and worry will rear their ugly heads. Just taking a few moments to tidy up can calm you down immeasurably. File stuff that needs filing, open your post (don't just ignore it) and check those bank statements. Also, create special areas for things – invest in a key rack so you don't spend twenty minutes every morning hunting for them; get yourself a folder for all your receipts; keep all your gig tickets in one drawer. Simple things that will save you time, money and head-space.

2 Make lists

You can't beat a good list. The very act of writing things down makes them more 'official' and gives your memory a jolt. Also, being able to tick things off a to-do list can keep up momentum and motivate you.

✦ Have a designated place for your lists, perhaps in a notebook or on your phone. There's nothing more annoying – or stressful – than making a list and then losing it

✦ Split the list into sections so it doesn't look overwhelming: 'Today', 'Tomorrow', 'Next week' etc. Then force yourself to only focus on the 'Today' one

✦ Break down big jobs into smaller ones. For example, if you have to write a ten chapter thesis on the global-economic crisis and you haven't started yet, don't put 'write thesis' on the list – that would be terrifying and very counter-productive. Instead break it down into sections: 'write introduction', 'write Chapter 1', and so on. The list will be longer, but it'll be much easier to tackle and you'll feel a sense of satisfaction in getting through it

✦ Don't avoid the scary stuff. Putting 'write blog' then 'wrap presents' followed by 'write presentation for CEO' is just giving you permission to procrastinate. Put the list in order of importance, break it down into smaller bits and start the intimidating stuff first. This way, getting to 'write blog' will feel like a reward

✦ For big things that are causing you lots of stress, allocate how much time you're going to spend on them. If it's an on-going project give yourself, say, three hours a day on it and write this down on your list so it's official. When that time is up you can blitz through the smaller things. Giving yourself a time slot will mean you're more likely to actually get on with it because there's an end point

✦ Update the list before you go to bed each night giving you peace of mind that you haven't forgotten anything

✦ If you genuinely have too much to do then write 'ask for help' on your list and then do it. Often we put off asking for help until the very last minute, causing ourselves more stress in the long-run

3 Take on less

Humans are social creatures and we generally want people to like us. We try to avoid conflict and don't like letting other people down. Those who don't give a damn about what others think tend not to feel as stressed as the rest of us. However, not caring can ultimately make you feel isolated. It's important to find a middle ground and care about the things that matter. We often take on more than we should. Learning to be assertive about what you can and can't do can save you loads of hassle. You can say no to people without offending them.

+ **Be more realistic about your time:** Say no to things you know you can't fit in, and be honest about why. Most people would much prefer you to say no than to promise to deliver something you can't

+ **Delegate:** We all know sometimes it's easier to do everything yourself, but you should trust people to be able to follow your instructions. In the long-term it'll pay off as they'll have a chance to learn and eventually you won't have to keep a beady eye on everything they do

+ **Question why you're doing stuff:** 'Why did I say I'd look after my friend's cat when I'm allergic?' If you can reasonably accomplish what you've agreed to then great, but if you can't then the likelihood is you won't meet your goals or you'll near enough kill yourself trying to. If this sounds like you then explain the situation to whoever you're frightened of letting down and work out a compromise

+ **Prioritise tasks that are within your control:** We know stress is exacerbated by things you feel you can't control so do the stuff you can first (i.e. pay a bill online before checking your email to see if that important response you're waiting for has arrived yet). You'll feel more able to face the stuff you can't control when you're feeling good about completing something else successfully

+ **Be honest about when you can deliver something:** There's no point saying, 'I can have that to you by Wednesday' if you know you don't have a cat in hell's chance of pulling it off. Saying, 'I can only get this to you in a fortnight' will save you a lot of bother and guilt

+ **Don't put yourself under too much pressure or feel you have to live up to other people's expectations:** For example, don't force yourself to go to a party that you have no interest in attending just because all your friends are going

+ **Work out what is most useful or interesting to you and focus on that:** If you're offered several projects but can only pick one, choose the one that you'll learn the most from, that will advance your career and that you'll enjoy doing

4 Schedule in some fun

Schedule things you actually like doing into your diary. Often we get so caught up in stress that we forget life is meant to be enjoyable. We'll relegate fun to the 'not important' list, which is terrible. Doing things you love will calm you down and make you happy. You'll be better able to face stress when it happens because you've given yourself a break.

5 Don't put stuff off

Procrastination can create huge levels of stress. Putting things off reduces your confidence in your ability to face the issue and makes it harder to get started. The problem increases in size and your refusal to deal with it makes you feel guilty and exacerbates the stress. It's a complicated issue which is why we've dedicated a whole chapter to it (see Chapter 9), but please note that just starting to tackle whatever it is will bring your anxiety levels down.

How to turn mountains into molehills

Control is a funny thing. Some people believe that what happens to them is guided by fate, God, luck or circumstance, while others believe it's dictated by their own choices. Whatever your belief system, we tend to cope much better with things if we know what's going on and can predict what's going to happen. Once you know what you're dealing with you often feel calmer, even when the situation is quite bad. For example, you'll probably feel calmer knowing that your constant migraines are caused by your bad eyesight, rather than having no idea why you keep getting them. Or, if you're stuck on a raft that's drifting out to sea, you'll feel calmer knowing your friend has alerted the coastguard.

When you're faced with something difficult and the outcome is a mystery you not only feel stressed, but often you'll start generating worst-case scenarios ('it will never work'). You're turning a molehill into a mountain – a habit you need to break.

ⓢ Our mountain to molehill guide

The fundamental way of feeling more in control is to take action. Rather than worrying and going over and over possible outcomes, just do something about it and make a start. Below is our step-by-step guide to making problems more manageable (with an example underneath each stage).

1 Identify the specific problem you want to deal with and write down, clearly, what's bothering you.

My sister is coming over tomorrow to pick up her laptop ... which I've broken.

2 Brainstorm as many solutions as you can in five minutes, writing down anything that comes to mind, even if it's ridiculous. Ask yourself what advice you would give to a friend in the same situation or actually ask a friend for advice – they may offer a different perspective.

   a Go out and pretend I forgot she was coming over.
   b Hand it back without telling her it's broken.
   c Confess and accept her inevitable (shouted) reprimand.
   d Tell her 'someone else broke it and I didn't realise until now'.
   e Apologise and offer to get it fixed.

3 Go over your list and evaluate the pros and cons of each idea. Don't just focus on how many there are (i.e. five pros, four cons), but how realistic they each are. After you've done this, star the most important points – both good and bad. (We've used a. as an example, but you'll need to do it for each of your solutions).

Pros: I won't have to face her*/I'll have more time to think of a plan
Cons: She won't have anything to work on/I'll feel even worse*/I'm just delaying the inevitable*/She won't have time to find an alternative computer or get it fixed*.

4 Choose the solution that answers your biggest concerns. There is often more than one way to solve a problem, but go with the one that you feel most comfortable with. Don't worry if it doesn't work, you can always try another idea – the main point here is that you're taking action and being proactive.
Have chosen to merge options c and e.

5 Break the solution down into achievable smaller steps. Think about what you'll need to do, how, where and when you'll do it. Also, note down whether anyone else needs to be involved. If there's a stage of the idea that is causing problems, then try to find a way round it – even if it means talking to a friend. (Admitting to people that you need help can be terrifying, but it's amazing how much better you'll feel.) Breaking things down into small steps will hopefully throw up some simple ways of making changes.
Ask her in. Make her a cup of tea. Hand her the laptop. Admit it's broken and tell her how it happened. Say sorry. Be ready to accept criticism and blame. Offer to try to get it fixed.

6 Get started. Once you've actually put the first part of your plan into action you'll feel more motivated to see it through and to make it work. If possible rehearse or try out your chosen solution – get a

friend to pretend to be your sister or just practice what you're going to say out loud if finding the right words is important.
Have texted her asking her to come over at 6p.m. tonight.

7 Evaluate how it went. If it bombed then go back to your brainstorm and try something else or start the process again using what you know now as a jumping-off point (i.e. the issue is now that your sister is furious and not speaking to you), but assess why it didn't work and remember to give yourself some credit for having a go. If it worked then remember to congratulate yourself. Rewarding yourself will make you more likely to look for solutions to other problems.
She was upset, but accepted my offer to get it fixed. She even said she'd go halves as it was old anyway.

Just by reading this guide you've taken proactive steps to deal with your stress and you should be proud of yourself. Facing a problem is tough and looking for ways around it is very positive. Even if nothing comes of your ideas, just thinking about trying to sort stuff out rather than hiding from it or panicking will make you feel calmer. Also, don't get despondent if your ideas don't work. Trying things out is often the best way to settle on a good plan.

Ⓢ Postponing panic

Stress can leap out of nowhere and attack you during the day, usually when it's least convenient. However, it often creeps up on people at night: it's harder to distract yourself while lying in bed staring at the ceiling. This can lead to insomnia and if there's one thing that sends stress levels through the roof it's exhaustion.

Setting aside a specific time to think about the things that you find stressful can stop you freaking out when you're trying to work, socialise or sleep. Knowing you are just postponing those thoughts rather than trying to ban them altogether can make it easier to disengage. Postponing works better than trying not to think about something at all. If we said, 'Don't you dare, under any circumstances, picture a pink elephant,' it's near enough impossible not to picture a pink elephant. Whereas, if you said to yourself, 'I can think about pink elephants later,' it's far easier to dismiss the thought for now. When you find yourself feeling anxious throughout the day just ask yourself, 'What am I achieving now by worrying?' and then file it away for later. You'll be far more likely to think about the problem in a proactive way if you haven't spent all day and all night worrying about it.

Here are some stress management techniques to try over the next week:

+ Set aside a specific time each day when you're going to think about what's making you feel stressed or anxious. It'll ease your mind knowing you're not avoiding thinking about it – you're just waiting until the designated time. How much time is up to you and can vary day to day, but the minimum should be fifteen minutes
+ Whenever you catch yourself worrying, tell yourself you're not going to think about it now. Be strict on postponing the stress-induced thoughts – don't just wade into them because once you're absorbed it's very hard to get back out. Stressful thoughts are like quicksand so once you realise you're thinking about them stop,

postpone them until later and refocus your mind to the present
moment or think about something else

+ At the designated time sit down somewhere and note down all the
things you've been stressed about

+ Write down possible solutions – anything that comes into your
head. (Use the mountain to molehill technique if you have time, if
not just note down some ideas.)

+ Stop at the end of the allotted time and list anything you want to
remember for tomorrow

+ When you're in bed remind yourself that you're in the middle of
making a plan and that you have time set aside to go through it the
next day

+ Keep a notepad by your bed in case any new thoughts pop into your
head while you're trying to sleep. Start thinking of your bed as a
place to sleep, not to worry. You can worry about it tomorrow!

Don't panic if these techniques didn't work for you straight away –
keep at it and also keep working through the mountain to molehill
routine for bigger troubles. The more you practise the quicker thoughts
like, 'I can think about that later,' will pop into your head when you're
feeling stressed. Hopefully, by the time your allotted fifteen minutes
to panic has rolled around you won't even need it – often delaying
thinking about small worries makes them redundant as whatever
you were worrying about has been resolved by then. 'Was she mad
about that email?' has turned into, 'Of course she wasn't mad about
that email,' as you've already received a reply. You'll also be better able
to identify and challenge common worrying thoughts and themes

because you're not letting them creep in and take root unnoticed.

Sometimes it takes stepping back from a problem and viewing it objectively to see how ridiculous it is. And even if it is a proper. genuine problem worthy of your worry, postponing thinking about it can give you the distance you need to come back to it with a calmer mind set. Even if you don't have any direct control over a situation you can control how you deal with it. Realising this and taking positive proactive action will automatically make whatever you're facing less intimidating, making you feel calmer.

Thoughts to take away

✓ Getting rid of any unnecessary demands will give you more time and energy to spend on genuine issues

✓ Facing up to problems and making plans for dealing with them will make you feel more in control of the situation

✓ Scheduling an allocated time to think about stress will take the pressure off and save you lots of time in the long run

What If You Stopped Thinking 'What If'?

Worry, stress and anxiety are like disorderly and exasperating triplets, with worry often acting as the ringleader. This chapter examines what worry is and how to distract yourself from its attention-seeking ways.

What is worry?

Worry is one of the thought processes behind stress and anxiety. Specifically, it's what you think when you're stressed about the possibility of something happening in the future. (Rumination is when you dwell on stuff that happened in the past.)

Like stress and anxiety, worry is natural – everybody does it. And also just like stress and anxiety it can be positive, if it helps you to figure ways out of sticky situations. However, it becomes problematic when instead of directing you towards a brilliant solution that saves

The three types of worry

What ifs: When you dwell on potential problems that don't exist yet. You imagine worst-case scenarios that you'll most likely never have to deal with: 'What if I fail my exam?' 'What if I don't make my deadline?' 'What if we break up?'

Concerns out of your control: When you worry about stuff you are powerless to change, like the weather or aging. Unlike 'what ifs' these issues actually exist, but you can't do anything about them.

Concerns within your control: When a problem exists that you do have some control over. For example, say you've lost a USB stick with sensitive work data on it. Worry about this type of issue can drive you to be proactive: you can retrace your steps, call various lost property departments, find out if there were any copies, etc.

the day it just makes you feel worse. Worry can also trigger the fight or flight response, leading to all the physical, behavioural and emotional problems associated with that state.

Typical themes that provoke these negative thoughts include: health (your own and other people's), relationships, work, finances, chores and responsibilities. However, excessive worry is normally associated with perfectionism – wanting things to go according to the plan you have mapped out in your head and worrying when you feel you're not meeting your own exacting standards.

If you are a natural worrier (and many people are), your internal threat detector – which decides how anxious you should feel about a situation – might be more finely tuned than someone who is more laid back. Don't worry though (see what we did there?) worrying this much is a habit and any habit can be broken.

What ifs

'What ifs' are the most common and most destructive of the three types of worry, which is why we're focusing on them in this chapter. Worrying about stuff that could happen, but hasn't yet and probably never will is the most monumental waste of time. And the worst part is that worrying about a possible future event triggers exactly the same response in your body as if it's actually happened. You're so busy picturing the worst-case scenario that you're living through those emotions – the panic at failing an exam, the horror of being dumped, the fear of losing your job. You're actually forcing yourself to experience the very thing you're scared of experiencing.

'What ifs' are like a vacuum cleaner – sucking up not only all of your time, but also the space in your head that's needed to think about other things. You end up losing concentration at work or at home leading to even more 'what ifs' about the things you've let slip. It can turn into a vicious circle, as illustrated below.

You're forcing yourself to go through the emotional wringer twice (if the event you're worrying about does happen) or feeling it needlessly (if it doesn't). For instance, imagine you send the guy you're dating a really angry text message after a few drinks. The next day you're so ashamed and embarrassed you turn your phone off because you don't want to see his reply. You spend the whole day feeling sick with worry over what he might write in response. 'What if he dumps me?' 'What if he laughs at me?' You can't concentrate, you're fidgety and your stomach feels like a locked box. Also, you've really inconvenienced yourself by turning off your phone – missing calls and messages from other people too. When you finally do turn your phone on you discover he's sent you a lovely message acknowledging you had every right to be angry and asking you out again. You've spent the whole day worrying about absolutely nothing. However, even if his reply was as horrible as you'd anticipated you have gained nothing by spending the whole day imagining it. You're still going to feel shocked and sad – the same emotions you've been going through all day.

Below is a mind map to illustrate what happens when you get

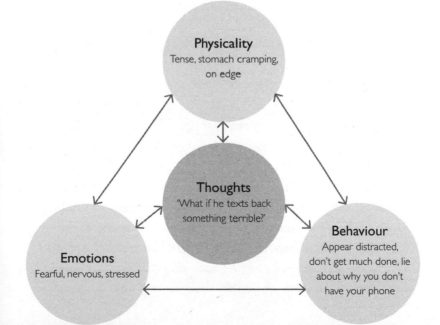

stuck on 'what if' thoughts and how they can affect your emotions, your behaviour and how you feel physically. (We've used the texting example above.)

⑤ Tackling your 'what ifs'

We'd like you to fill in your own mind map now using our example for guidance. Try to be very specific – what exactly was your most troubling 'what if' thought and how did this make you feel emotionally and physically and what did it make you do or think about doing? Filling it in should make you realise how destructive these thoughts are and how the negativity spirals. You can stop the cycle though by:

Interrupting your physical response: Practice the relaxation exercises in Chapter 3.

Interrupting your thoughts: Distract yourself. (Read on to find out how.)

Concerns out of your control

These kind of worries are as big a waste of time as 'what ifs', but they're not as destructive because there isn't the same guilt attached to them. Worrying about the weather or getting older is totally useless (you're not going to stop either the rain or time by wishing it), but they're not influenced by you, whereas 'what if' scenarios are normally viewed as directly attributable to something you've done or played a part in.

If you are torturing yourself with thoughts like, 'I can't believe it's been fifteen years since I left university,' or 'It's going to rain today which will ruin everything,' stop! You cannot control nature and it's not designed to wind you up. These things affect everybody. Again, if you're bothered by these sorts of thoughts you should try to relax yourself physically and distract yourself mentally.

Concerns within your control

Of the three categories of worry, this is the only one we'd advise you to spend any time thinking about because you can actually do something about it. These are concerns that you do have some power and influence over so they can be tackled by problem-solving strategies. For example, if you have an upcoming exam and are thinking, 'I'm not prepared for this – I'm going to fail', then you can revise. Or, if you're dreading seeing your cousin at a family event because you've had a row, you can call him and make peace. You can take proactive action to solve the issue or issues.

If any of these worries veer into 'what ifs' (e.g. 'What if I fail my exam?' or 'What if my cousin shouts at me?'), you can dismiss them out of hand because those are different concerns that don't exist yet so dwelling on them is pointless. You can then turn your attention back to the worry that does exist and that is within your control (e.g. not being prepared for your exam and having to face your cousin at the party).

⑤ Don't worry, be calm

The most basic ways of dealing with worry is to either forget about it (if it's out of your control) or do something about it (if it's within your control).

When you next find yourself worrying about something, ask yourself the following questions to determine which course of action you can take:

1 Notice the worry (don't just let it bubble away in the background, confront it).

2 Ask yourself, 'Can I do something about it?'

✦ If the answer is yes

a Make yourself an action plan: what, when and how are you going to address the problem? (You can use the mountain to molehill guide from the last chapter.)

b Schedule it. Actually note down when you're going to do it. Just saying, 'I'll deal with it later,' won't work.

✦ If the answer is no

a Let the worry go. Consciously decide to stop thinking about it.

b Change your focus of attention. Mentally wrench your thoughts away from the worry. If you find this hard then our distraction strategy below should help.

⑤ Weapons of mass distraction

Distraction is an effective strategy for dealing with 'what ifs' and 'concerns out of your control' – it is absolutely not advisable for worries you can influence and for which you need to take action. However, for stuff you can't do anything about that's taking up valuable brain space, distraction is brilliant. It works by shifting the focus of your attention away from both your negative thoughts and the physical sensations of stress and anxiety. It works because (as anyone who ever claims to multi-task knows) you can't truly focus on two things at once. Concentrating on something calming means you won't be concentrating on whatever's stressful (or at least you'll be concentrating much less on it).

Below are some tried and tested ways of distracting yourself. Some of them may sound obvious, but they work. Try each for at least three minutes, giving your mind time to switch off. After this the worries will have reduced. You may think of them again when you've finished, but giving yourself that respite will make you calmer and give you some distance from the thoughts.

Play a game: Take a break from whatever you're meant to be doing (which you're not doing anyway because you're worrying) and play a game. Go online, download an app onto your phone, check the newspaper for a puzzle or buy a puzzle book (don't be embarrassed, we all have them). Games demand your attention, but aren't over-taxing or stressful – nagging thoughts won't get a look in.

Find your own grounding object: Find something that reminds you of a calm or happy time – or just pick something new that you like. Keep it with you all the time. Just knowing it's there will make you feel safer and touching and looking at it can reduce anxiety.

Get physical: Do something – anything. Go for a walk, run, cycle. Tidy up, hang up the washing, look round the shops. Exercise has great natural benefits, but even just moving will mean you have to be aware of your surroundings, taking your mind off your thoughts. A change of scenery always eases worry (as long as you're not strolling into an ominously dark alleyway).

Listen to music: Music is a great stress reducer and is proven to reduce feelings of anxiety, steady your heart rate and lower your blood pressure. A favourite song or inspiring album can trigger memories and activate your imagination.

Read a good book: It doesn't matter what you're into, reading is an unbeatable escape. Whether you like blood-splattered thrillers or stories about fluffy cats, if you're fully involved in a book the real world will slip away. But take notice of those times when you suddenly realise you're on chapter 3 and you can't remember anything about the first two. It's easy to skim-read while your mind's elsewhere. Notice it and re-read them. There's no point pretending you're distracted if you're not.

Become more mindful: Mindfulness is all about becoming present in the moment and focusing outwards rather than inwards. You have to tune into your senses, becoming engaged in what you're doing and absorbed into the world around you rather than stuck in your head. Taking notice of where you are and what you're doing is such a simple way of unwinding … and it works.

✦ Look at everything around you and then concentrate on a specific detail – the texture of a woman's jacket, the colours in the graffiti on the wall, what the shops that you're walking past sell. Then take it further: try to guess what kind of person someone is, or who might have painted the graffiti and how long it would have taken

✦ Listen. Take notice of everything you can hear and try to work out where the sounds are coming from and what they are. Or listen to music, paying attention to the lyrics or trying to identify different instruments, changes in pace, etc. Download a podcast you think might interest you. There are lots of ways to stop listening to your own thoughts

✦ Feel. Keep something in your pocket that has a specific texture – like wood or wool. Touch it and talk yourself through how it feels, using it as a prompt to remind yourself to concentrate on the world around you, rather than your thoughts. If you imbue meaning into an object it will trigger something within your mind, i.e. when you brush that piece of wool with your fingertips it'll trigger the memory of your putting it there for that reason, instantly making you feel calmer

Email a friend: Only write down the positive things you've been doing. This will make you feel better and prompt you to acknowledge that there are good things happening which deserve your attention too.

Phone a pal: Talking to someone is immediately distracting – if you force yourself to concentrate on what they're saying and don't just wait for your turn to speak or mull on your own issues. It reminds you that there's life going on outside of your head. Just hearing a friendly voice can make you feel better – and laughter is a proven mood-booster. You can't be roaring with laughter while torn up with anxiety (unless you're hysterical). There is almost always a funny side to every worry – the best tonic to your deepest irrational anxieties is to air them and have a good laugh in the process. Also, often hearing about other people's problems can make you feel less bad about yours. Being reminded that you're not the only one experiencing stress can make you feel less lonely.

See your friends: Often when people feel stressed they sacrifice socialising, feeling as if they don't have time or that they won't be good company. This is rubbish. Social support is an integral part of feeling calmer and actual physical human contact (as opposed to just texting, emailing or calling) is so important, fending off feelings of isolation. Also, you don't have to chat about your worries if you don't want to – just being in company with people you like will take your mind off them.

Surf the net: Spend some time tracking down blogs you're interested in, finding old mates on Facebook, or searching for a holiday you'd like to go on. Genuinely mindless things. (It's called mindless for a reason – it's giving your head a break.)

Learn something new: You concentrate harder when you're trying to digest new information so look into taking up a new hobby, learning a new recipe or try researching something you're interested in.

Read positive quotes: Okay, this may sound cheesy, but writing down inspiring and motivating quotes somewhere you can access them easily when you're feeling stressed can really help to calm you down. Whether they're funny, profound or provocative, quotes can become personal mantras making you feel more positive.

Even if you don't think some of these suggestions are for you, give all of them a go at least once – you might scoff at the idea of mindfulness, but later discover you're actually very good at it. You might think you hate card games, but discover a flair for them. Often we dismiss things that sound too simple or too different to what we're used to. The whole point of reading this book is to change what you're doing at the moment – because it's not working for you.

Also, don't wait until you're really stressed before trying out some of these things – start straight away. It's much harder to concentrate when you're panicking so if you've already got into the habit of phoning a friend or playing a game during your tea break you'll know what to do straight away when you really do need distracting, and stepping out of your routine will come more naturally.

Thoughts to take away

✓ Don't waste your time worrying about 'what ifs' or things you can't control

✓ Plan a strategy for dealing with worries you can control and then take action

✓ Distraction is an excellent way of minimising the negative effect of worries you can't do anything about

7

Putting Worry in Its Place

We've covered how we worry – examining the different ways we dwell on fears about the future when we're stressed – so now it's time to look at why we worry. By recognising what's prompting those thoughts you'll be able to stop them early on.

Why do we worry?

The last chapter proved that dwelling on 'what ifs' and things we can't influence is pointless – so why do we all do it? While distraction is an excellent technique for managing time-wasting concerns, for any kind of long-term change it's essential to understand why you're worrying so you'll naturally do it less.

Worry is linked to temperament and upbringing – it's a learned response that you were either born with or developed in your childhood as a way of dealing with stress and anxiety. How much you worry and what you worry about is totally dependent on you as an individual. Commonly, all worriers believe dwelling on those thoughts is somehow positive. By identifying your reasons for worrying and by questioning whether it is in fact helpful, you can decide whether you

The three main justifications for worrying

Responsibility: You view worry as a positive personality trait as you think it shows you care. Also, you believe not worrying about something is more likely to cause a negative outcome.

Control: Worrying makes you feel more in control of a situation and more confident about the choices and decisions you're going to make. By thinking it over and over you can be prepared for the worst happening, while giving yourself the best chance to get things right.

Motivation: You believe worrying motivates you to get stuff done.

want to continue thinking this way and when you decide you don't
(we're confident you'll want to change after trying our strategies)
you'll be able to scrap pointless worry from your life altogether.

By believing any or all of these justifications you've managed to
make worrying a positive thing – when 99 per cent of the time it's
not. The remaining 1 per cent covers the times when it does actually
prompt you to solve a problem, however, even that's generous because
no doubt the problem could have been solved without you worrying
about it. You have to challenge these beliefs you have about worry to
realise it's rarely helpful, enabling you to create new genuinely positive
thinking processes.

Challenging worry as a form of 'responsibility'

1 'Worrying shows I care'

It's common to believe that worrying shows you care – and to a
certain extent this is true. If you didn't give a damn about something
you definitely wouldn't be worried about it. However, it's essential to
recognise that worrying and caring are two totally different entities:
worrying is negative and caring is positive. They're not interchangeable
and they're not the same thing. The symptoms of worry (feeling
stressed, anxious and on edge, behaving out of character and feeling
physically tense) are not the same as the symptoms of caring about
something or someone (feeling fulfilled, doing things for other people,
feeling physically fine).

Ⓢ Unpicking the belief

✦ List in your notebook the things you're worrying about under the guise of caring. For example, 'Worrying about mum's operation'. Write next to each an alternative way of proving both to yourself and to other people that you care, i.e. 'Send Mum a card, make time to visit, speak to the doctors myself.' This should help you prove to yourself that there are other more positive, proactive ways to care

+ Picture someone you know who's really laid–back. Do they still care about things? Of course they do, they just have different ways of showing it. Next time you find yourself freaking out ask yourself, 'What would [insert name of chilled-out person here] do?'

+ Turn the belief into a positive: 'Okay, I'm worrying, which shows I care, so now what can I do about it?' Acknowledge the worry, stop it and move on to a positive action

2 'Worrying prevents bad stuff from happening'

Believing that worrying will prevent a bad outcome is Grade-A nonsense, most likely based upon a one-off event or driven by perfectionism or a fear of failure. If you once aced an exam which you'd been worrying about and then spectacularly flunked another that you hadn't been worried about at all, then it's perhaps inevitable you'll land on worry as the deciding factor. That you didn't revise enough for the second exam or studied the wrong things (clearly the real reasons why you failed) will only exacerbate the 'care' factor too: 'I didn't care enough about the exam so I deserved to fail.'

Ⓢ Interrogate the belief

+ Make a list of things that have gone well recently, e.g. a date, a job interview, a family dinner, etc. Note down on a scale of 1–10 how much you worried about them (1 being 'not at all' and 10 being 'lots') and be honest. We'll bet there are a few things on that list that went well despite you not worrying about them

✦ Write down 'THOUGHTS DON'T HAVE MAGICAL POWERS' in your notebook and read it when you next find yourself worrying about the outcome of something. Your thoughs can't influence events either positively or negatively – you can't think your way into a promotion, just like you can't think your way out of it. Thinking about winning the lottery isn't going to increase your chances of scooping the jackpot just as thinking about closing that door isn't going to make it close. You know all of this is true, so why are you convinced thinking about your problems or issues will change them? It won't. It's what you do that alters outcomes

Challenging worry as a form of 'control'

There are three parts to this belief.

1 'Worrying makes me feel more in control'

When you have no control over a situation it's natural to want to try to exert some. But, as we discussed in the last chapter, you can't do anything about 'what ifs' as the situation doesn't exist yet (and probably never will exist) and you can't invent influence over something that's totally out of your hands like aging or the weather.

ⓢ Confront the belief

✦ Ask yourself: 'Can I actually control the outcome of this situation?' If the answer is no then stop worrying (use the distraction techniques from Chapter 6). You have to accept the things you cannot influence.

If the answer is yes then do something about it (using the mountain to molehill strategy in Chapter 5). Worrying is not the same thing as taking action

✦ Write down your biggest worry about the situation and then assess if there might have been a smaller original worry that snowballed. For example, 'What if I break up with my boyfriend?' could easily have started out as, 'What if my boyfriend gets angry that I embarrassed him?' Your biggest worry here is breaking up with your boyfriend, but that's spiralled from a simple fear about making a fool of yourself. Realising this should flag up how destructive thoughts actually make you feel less in control than you did in the beginning. You need to challenge the original worry to fix the second, bigger worry. Why would you make a fool of yourself? Why would your boyfriend care? If he cares what does that say about him? etc

2 Worry is an effective problem-solving device and makes me feel more certain about my choices

This is when the doubtful part of your brain starts questioning your instincts. Imagine you're on *Who Wants to Be a Millionaire?* and you're asked a question that you know the answer to ... then the host asks, 'Are you sure?' and suddenly you're not. You've convinced yourself that by worrying you're helping yourself become more certain and giving yourself more options, when in reality you're just undermining your own decision-making capabilities.

⑤ Face up to the belief

✦ Write down 'DOUBT BREEDS DOUBT' in your notebook and read it whenever you find yourself questioning your gut reactions. Assessing your options calmly is not the same as questioning yourself to the point where you lose any sense of what you want to do. Uncertainty is neither positive nor negative as you don't know the outcome yet. Just because you can't predict the future doesn't mean that the future will be bad, yet worrying about it will always give things a negative spin. What's causing you anxiety and making you feel negative is how you're undermining your own decision-making skills. Have some faith in yourself!

✦ Write down all the pros and cons about a decision you need to make, assessing them calmly and rationally – or ask a friend or family member to run through your choices with you

✦ If you don't have all the information you need to make an informed decision then wait until you do. Worrying about uncertainty is futile

3 'Worrying will prepare me for (and protect me from) a bad outcome'
You reckon that by worrying you're whittling away the chances of being blindsided by disaster. That belief should have been scuppered in the last chapter; worrying about something that hasn't happened yet is pointless and if the worst does happen you've just insured you'll experience the horrible emotions twice.

⑤ Scrap the belief

✦ Get rid of the 'If I expect the worst I won't ever be disappointed' approach to life. If something bad happens you'll still feel crappy, whether you'd anticipated it or not. Constantly thinking negatively will make you behave negatively – which might actually make you influence events negatively. It's a self-fulfilling prophecy. Rewrite the story with a positive outcome. You'll feel more hopeful which will in turn make you behave more positively, putting you in a much better position to influence events in a good way

✦ Ask yourself, 'If the worst does happen will it matter in a day, a month or year?' We bet 99 per cent of the time the answer is no, but for that 1 per cent when the answer is yes there's no point moping – the only way to minimise the effect is to tell yourself you'll make proactive plans if it does happen

Challenging worry as a form of 'motivation'

'Worry motivates me to get stuff done'

This is one of the most common misconceptions about worry – that it drives us to succeed and to push for what we want. The fundamental problem with this is that worry actually only slows us down and makes us question our decisions (as discussed previously). The 'getting stuff done' part can proceed much better without all that worrying holding it up.

ⓢ Challenge the belief

✦ Give yourself a pep talk – out loud if that helps. If your friend asked you for motivation, would you list all possible disastrous outcomes? Of course you wouldn't – yet that's what you're doing to yourself! Give yourself credit for things you've done well and for how far you've come. Not only do humans thrive on praise, but it'll serve as a reality check to snap you out of negative thinking. Note down the sayings below somewhere you can easily access them then, whenever you're feeling negative, find the one that relates to your situation and repeat it to yourself several times:

+ It's not the end of the world
+ It's their problem, not mine
+ I handled that well
+ Who knows, I might actually enjoy it
+ I can cope with this

+ I can deal with this – I have before
+ I'm getting better
+ It'll be easier next time
+ At least I learned something

For one day whenever you catch yourself worrying make a note of how long you think you've been worrying for. At the end of the day add up how much time you spent doing nothing. This should prove to you what a waste of time worrying is so the next time you catch yourself doing it you can stop and start doing something more positive. As soon as you actually start a project all those anxious predictions you've been making will stop.

Thoughts to take away

✓ Don't mistake worry for taking action

✓ Thoughts can't influence the future – what you do can

✓ You can feel motivated, in control and show you care without worry holding you back

Reality
Check

How you interpret an event determines how stressed you get. This chapter looks at ways of thinking realistically and calmly about angst-inducing situations.

Negative automatic thoughts (NATs)

Worry is just one aspect of negative thinking surrounding stress – an important one, but not the only one. Ultimately, how stressed you feel about an event is determined by how you interpret a situation and whether your primary and secondary appraisals are negative – which are all determined by your thoughts.

Thoughts are ridiculously fast – like cheetahs sprinting across your brain. Because we're thinking all the time we barely take any notice of humdrum thoughts or things we accept as facts. This is where Negative Automatic Thoughts (NATs) come in. NATs are ingrained thoughts that loiter just below the level of consciousness. Whenever they appear you accept them without challenging them or even really noticing them. These thoughts affect your ideas and beliefs and how you view yourself. When you feel anxious and your fight or flight response kicks in your mind automatically becomes focused on the 'threat' meaning NATs such as, 'I can't handle this,' are allowed to run riot through your head unchecked.

When you're under siege from NATs, certain biases come into play that distort information or bend it to fit your fears, leaving you far more likely to interpret pretty much everything negatively and allow small things to be blown out of proportion.

To have any chance of managing your stress levels it's absolutely essential to question your NATs and acknowledge that most of them are nonsense. You'll then be able to formulate credible alternatives (that your negative mind will grudgingly accept) – this will make you feel calmer, happier and more in control.

NATs in a nutshell

NATs are streams of appraisals and interpretations that run through your head. They can be conscious and deliberate, but often they're automatic so you're not even aware of them – you accept them and file them away as statements of fact. For example, 'I'm going to miss a definitive milestone in our friendship by not attending my mate's hen do.' They're easy to accept as they can often be plausible (there's a chance you will miss out on some memorable moments), but they're always unreasonable and unrealistic (you've missed key moments in each other's lives before and it didn't affect your friendship).

When you're stressed and have become a master at generating worst-case scenarios in your head, you don't ever challenge NATs, which is terrible because if you did you'd realise they don't stand up to scrutiny. The more you believe and accept negative thoughts the worse you're going to feel – they'll go from being hurtful, to acceptable, to obvious. 'Of course I'll miss out on important stuff. She'll come back much closer to her other friends and I'll be resented for my absence.' This can make you feel angry, frustrated and sad.

ⓢ Friendly advice

When you next identify a NAT or find yourself hunting down proof to back up a negative view ask yourself, 'What advice would I give to a friend if she were going through or thinking the same thing? Are these thoughts rational? Is there a positive to find here?' You're far more likely to be fairer to a friend than yourself and trying to find a balanced view is the definition of fair.

How we process things

When your alarm goes off in the morning you don't talk yourself though every little thing that you do: 'I'm going to put my feet on the floor and push myself up, stretch, check my phone, walk to the shower, etc.' You just get up and do what you normally do because you're on autopilot. This is down to 'processing' – how we manage all the thoughts in our head in an efficient way. Our brain chooses what's important to think about and what's not, siphoning off any information it considers inconsequential. This is integral to our being able to function properly because if we had to really think about every tiny thing we did our brains would beg for mercy.

This system works well – until your brain switches to negative autopilot and chooses to only focus on the bad stuff, filtering all information negatively. Other useful and relevant facts are missed or ignored, meaning your anxiety levels are maintained or increased. Your memory also plays a dastardly role, recalling only instances in your past that back up your negative viewpoint. This is exactly what happens when your body goes into fight or flight mode – your mind is trained only to pick up on things that can be construed as threatening, leaving

Example: James's judgement

James had admitted to his closest friend, Simon, over a series of emails that he thought Simon's sister, Lisa, was treating him badly. She belittled Simon in public and constantly put him down in front of his friends. Simon hadn't replied to his email and James was feeling anxious about it. After another day of silence he was convinced he'd crossed a line and Simon was furious with him.

James emailed a couple of other friends to find out if they'd heard from Simon and some of them had so he was obviously online and receiving emails. He hunted on Facebook to see if Simon had left any updates and discovered he'd written 'Families are complicated' the day before.

As far as James was concerned this was cast-iron proof that Simon was giving him the silent treatment. He concluded that Simon was furious with him. He totally ignored the fact that a lot of his friends hadn't heard from Simon and he also ignored how Simon had written something else equally cryptic about his family a week before he'd sent the email.

In reality, Simon just needed some time to assess how to reply. He was grateful that James cared, but also felt a bit embarrassed about Lisa's behaviour and wasn't sure how to deal with it. He'd definitely reply to James soon though as he knew he'd be worried.

you believing:
+ The likelihood of a feared event is higher than it really is
+ The impact of the event is worse than it really it is
+ You can't cope

You'll also read totally neutral events negatively. Your body thinks it's facing a life or death situation so wants you to be prepared for any possible danger.

When suffering from this type of bias your mind is actually trying to help you out by singling out evidence of 'threats' that back up your negative view (i.e. that Simon had been in touch with other friends and had written cryptically on Facebook), but in reality it couldn't be less helpful. People who feel stressed or anxious will often jump to the worst conclusion, totally disregarding any evidence to the contrary. James actually has no definitive proof that Simon is angry with him and by jumping to conclusions he's ignoring the facts: he doesn't know how Simon feels about his email or what he's going to do. He can only wait to hear back from him or take proactive action by messaging or calling him to ask how he feels. Worrying and dwelling on it is pointless, time-consuming and damaging.

Ⓢ Don't look, don't find

Over the next three days, take note of all the 'For Sale' signs you see on buildings. Don't try and look for them – if you happen to see one, make a mental note of it and a general approximation of how many you've seen altogether at the end of each day. Then, for the following three days, actively look for the signs. If you see one, make a physical note of it so you can keep track of them as you go. At the end of each day, tally up the total number of signs you saw.

You will no doubt have seen lots more signs in the second set of three days than the first. This isn't because hundreds have suddenly appeared overnight, it's because you were actively hunting them out in the second set of days, just like you actively hunt out negative 'threats' or 'evidence' when you're feeling stressed. This doesn't mean the negative things are more meaningful than the positive or that they're factual – it just means you've altered what you're paying attention to. If you're buying a new sofa you'll suddenly notice everyone's sofa when you go to their houses. If you're buying a new phone, you'll look at everyone's phone. These things haven't gained in importance – you're just giving them priority in your head.

What you choose to pay attention to will also be determined by your natural biases. Everyone's a little bit biased about stuff. You're brought up with certain beliefs and however objective you try to be, your biases will creep in and colour how you think – like when you support a football team or a political party. However, your beliefs can change and then your biases will change, which is good because at the moment there's a whole lot of bias going on in your head that needs changing. When you're stressed you'll feel very strongly about things you previously didn't give a damn about. Suddenly totally innocuous events and occurrences become relatable to you. That whispered conversation at the back of the office? That was about you. That loud laugh in the gym? That was about you. The fact that none of your friends have replied to your group email yet? That's about you. These biases will create and shape your NATs.

The good news is that once you get better at noticing your biases and NATs you'll be able to distance yourself from them and challenge them.

Common types of NAT

1 Jumping to conclusions

This is when you draw a conclusion from insufficient evidence (like James did). This kind of thinking also affects your view of the future – you'll start predicting what other people are thinking and what they're going to do because you suddenly believe you can read minds.

S The Pie of Truth

Step 1 Draw a large circle on a piece of paper. Next to it write a list of all of the possible outcomes of an event, leaving the most dire and eye-wateringly horrific until last. Here's an example:

The Event: I misunderstood a news story and wrote a comment on Twitter about it that was, on reflection, really stupid. Several people I know and a few strangers corrected me publicly.

Step 2 Make a pie-chart by allocating a section (or a percentage) of the circle to each outcome based on how probable you think it is or how probable a friend would think it was (either ask a friend or ask yourself what you would tell a friend if they came to you). And be honest. By the time you've got to G. you'll no doubt have a tiny sliver of the circle – if anything – left. You'll be forced to admit that you're jumping to conclusions based on little to no evidence.

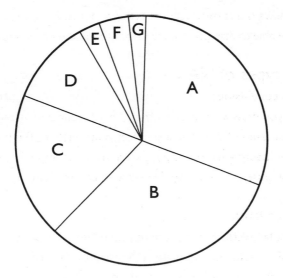

Possible outcomes (starting with the least bad)

A Everyone forgets about it within a day

B Most of my friends and colleagues don't notice

C I lose a couple of followers on the site

D I lose all credibility on the site and loads of people stop
following me

E People remember it for weeks and keep bringing it up

F Some really important people see it and think I'm an idiot

G It jeopardises my chances for a job as future employers see it
and think I'm stupid

2 Catastrophising

You hugely overestimate the chances of disaster and dwell on the worst possible outcome of a situation while underestimating your ability to cope. For example, you miss a deadline so assume you'll lose your job. Or you send an angry text to someone so write off your whole relationship.

⑤ Put it to the test

Ask yourself:

+ Am I catastrophising?
+ What truly is the worst that can happen?
+ What would be the best-case scenario?
+ What is, honestly and realistically, most likely to happen?
+ If the worst does happen, what can I do? What skills do I possess to help me deal with it?

3 The reverse binoculars

You exaggerate the importance of negative events and reduce the importance of those that don't back up your negative view. For example, you'll focus on all the times you've messed up before and completely ignore all the times you've succeeded. You filter out all positive information, storing only the negative stuff.

⑤ Play devil's advocate

Consciously hunt out opposing views. So, for example, if you think your boss scowled at you and all the evidence seemingly backs this up (she hasn't answered your emails; she didn't give you the credit you deserved in that meeting), then decide actively to look for things that conflicts with this belief. Did she scowl at other people too? Did she give anyone else credit in that meeting? Is she usually late replying to emails? Get perspective on a situation by asking someone who's not involved for their opinion. Note down all the times when you have succeeded in similar situations or when things have worked out much better than you thought they would. Acknowledging circumstances that don't match your negative assessments will give you a more balanced and realistic view and make you feel calmer even though your anxious mind's shouting, 'Run away, she hates you.' You need to kick-start your rational mind.

4 Shoulda, woulda, coulda

You worry about how things ought to be, how others perceive you and what you should be doing according to some unwritten rules in your head. You commonly overuse words like 'should', 'must' and 'can't' and your best is never good enough.

⑤ Ditch being judge and juror

Change 'should', 'must' and 'can't' to the far more flexible 'could' and 'will'. For example, 'I should have done that,' changes to, 'I could/will do that next time.' You need to give up your unrealistic internal demands that are based upon an idealised view of how things should be. Cutting yourself some slack and embracing more flexible beliefs will reduce stress if things go wrong.

5 Savour failure

Stressed people tend to dwell or ruminate on recollections of negative things that happened in the past. Musing on past events that didn't end well or had negative repercussions only makes you more fearful of the future, leading you to project a doom and gloom cast onto everything, like you're wearing grey-tinted glasses. It will undermine your confidence and stop you moving forward, taking risks and appreciating what you have.

Ⓢ Accept what you cannot change

Cut yourself some slack about the past. It's over – move on. Regret and recrimination won't help anyone. You made the best decision you could at the time based upon the information you had, otherwise you wouldn't have made it. Accept what has happened, learn from it and deal with what is actually happening now and what you do have some control over. Positive action will make you feel calmer.

Thoughts: prepare to duel

The strategies above are on-going general day-to-day tools that can be used to give yourself a reality check when you're feeling particularly stressed. On a more long-term basis you need to challenge NATs and your negative autopilot setting in order to fundamentally change how you think.

Ⓢ Fill in the table using the following questions opposite and suggested answers as a guide:

Date/time	Situation	Emotions and physical response	Anxious predictions? What thinking bias is this?	Alternative perspectives. Use the key questions to find other views of the situation	What is a more balanced view?
Thursday	Had an argument with my sister	Have a horrible knot in my stomach and feel guilty	She was already mad at me so won't speak to me for weeks and will moan about me to the rest of my family (jumping to conclusions and catastrophising)	She needs some time to think it over and to calm down. She'll eventually get in touch – she has before	She's probably angry and wants some space. She won't moan to my family as she's never done that before
Friday	Meeting at work about how I'm doing	Nervous, anxious, nauseous	They're going to say my work isn't good enough and they aren't going to renew my trial period because that's what happened at my last job (jumping to conclusions, catastrophising, savour failure)	I've been working hard since I started, I have had good feedback. I don't know yet how the meeting will go, but I have no reason to think the worst	They may have some constructive feedback and say I have areas to improve on, but overall I've been working hard. I hope that they make my job permanent

+ What happened?
+ How did you feel emotionally and physically?
+ What did you think might happen?
+ Are there any alternative perspectives? What evidence is there to support them?
+ Can you identify what kind of NATs you had from the list above?
+ Are you setting yourself an unobtainable or unrealistic standard?

+ Are you focusing only on negative so-called facts that aren't actually facts at all?
+ Are you over-estimating how responsible you are for the way things work out or how likely the event is?
+ Are you underestimating what you can do to deal with the problem?
+ What is most likely to happen?

Filling in the chart will have forced you to step back from the situation and view it objectively and rationally. It'll be obvious where different kinds of NATs are creeping in and you can now use the tools you have to challenge them. You'll also have to acknowledge where you accepted ambiguous presumptions as fact. In the example for Thursday we wrote 'She was already mad at me' as if it were an established truth. If our sister had called us a couple of days before and screamed, 'I'm really mad at you,' then that's fair enough, but if she hadn't why have we just stated it as fact? Often we brand the assumptions we're making as truths when they're only based on our beliefs and interpretations. Remember to always insert 'I think' at the start of thoughts like this, i.e. 'I think she was already mad at me'. This will prompt you to look for proof against the thought. Filling in this table and challenging your NATs using the strategies detailed will fundamentally change how you think and interpret events for the better.

Thoughts to take away

✓ Confronting your negative thoughts will make you feel calmer

✓ Force yourself to be fair and acknowledge the positive with the negative and challenge your assumptions

✓ NATs aren't uninvited – you've accepted them into your head so it's up to you to kick them out!

9

Stop Procrastinating ... NOW

This chapter is for all those people whose motto is either 'I'll do it later' or 'If I leave it for a bit maybe it'll go away'. Avoiding dealing with events or situations that are stressful will only make them more stressful. Here we explain how to make facing them doable rather than daunting.

I'll just do this first ...

What you both do and don't do to deal with a problem can hugely influence how stressful it is. Unfortunately when we get scared (through anxiety) about the probable outcome of something it's a common human trait to put it off or avoid it altogether. This covers everything from relatively small or trivial stuff: 'I'll write my party guest list tomorrow,' to huge life changing decisions: 'I won't quit my job to go to art school because I'm not good enough to get in.'

Stress reduces confidence and makes it harder to start things. When just the prospect of starting something is overwhelming you'll put it off for longer and longer until it gets bigger and scarier and eventually turns into a huge deal that either needs immediate attention (like the guest list) or that chips away at your self-esteem for years and years (the art-school dream) until you think it's too late.

The effects of avoidance

By avoiding something or putting it off, you're not giving yourself the opportunity to disprove your negative beliefs. Avoiding it seems easier at the time, but any relief you get at not dealing with it is very short-lived. Your discomfort may be reduced in the short-term, but you're instigating a far more damaging long-term slog – also adding guilt and regret into the mix. You'll feel bad that you didn't do what you wanted to do or that you needed to do and you'll berate yourself for it – which just makes the original problem seem more insurmountable. At this point your fight or flight response kicks in as whatever you're putting off becomes threatening and you feel you can't cope – resulting in a determination to avoid it at all costs. You're not only maintaining the levels of stress and anxiety you were at before, you're actively increasing them, as in the vicious circle below.

Situation or event you are avoiding

Feel under pressure and unable to start

Think, 'I'll deal with it later' or 'I can't think about it now'

Ignore it, do other things, distract yourself

Feel even more stressed and anxious, but now also guilty

Types of avoidance

We can find a million ways to try to block unwelcome situations or events from our minds, but below are some common avoidance strategies you might recognise:

+ Putting things off by doing other stuff, e.g. cleaning, phoning a friend, checking emails, etc.

+ Permanently using the distracting techniques listed in Chapter 5 to avoid dealing with worries you can control and could actually do something about, rather than for the ones you can't (like 'what ifs' or the weather)

+ Working so hard you don't have time for anything else

+ Never stopping – be it at work or socially – so you don't give yourself a chance to think

+ Using alcohol or drugs to block out the problem or situation

+ Comfort eating

+ Excessive exercise

+ Doing anything that avoids both the problem and thinking about the problem

Why we avoid certain things

There are loads of reasons why you might be avoiding something, but the main ones are usually:

+ A fear of failure

+ Fear of making the wrong choice or decision

+ Because you want to do things perfectly

+ A fear of losing control

+ A fear of change

+ Trying to avoid the possibility of more stress and anxiety
+ Because you don't have time (ironic really since you now have even less time after wasting lots procrastinating)

You might avoid starting an essay because you don't think you can do it, or avoid seeing a friend because you know you're going to have to discuss something that makes you uncomfortable, or avoid answering the phone in case someone's calling with bad news.

You might even put stuff off until the last minute to prove a point to yourself i.e. you don't think your essay or presentation will be good enough so if you rush it when you get bad grades you can blame it on not having spent enough time on it. Your fear of failure or of not measuring up is causing you to deliberately sabotage your chances. That way if you do fail you can always tell yourself if you had put more effort in you would have done better. It's the same with relationships. People can deliberately sabotage a relationship through a fear of rejection. That way if they do get rejected they have concrete behaviour to blame it on rather than having to look at the deeper issues. Doing this means you'll never have the chance to prove to yourself that you could have succeeded at the essay or the relationship if you had given them a fair shot.

Some people try to keep control through rituals such as constantly checking things, keeping everything in order or frequently asking for reassurance. This type of behaviour is often used as a procrastination tool, which can reduce anxiety in the short-term, but it doesn't deal with the actual problem and means when the anxiety inevitably comes back you have to start the rituals all over again, making it worse for you in the long-term.

By not entering a situation – or doing something half-heartedly – you won't ever get the chance to see how your anxiety would have naturally dropped if you'd faced it and seen it through. Anxiety can't stay at fever pitch forever and it's normally at its highest at the beginning of a task, so once you start facing the issue it will already be on its way down.

How to beat thought suppression

When you're avoiding something you'll be trying desperately to suppress your thoughts about it too. No matter how much you try to distract yourself, whatever you're avoiding will follow you about as relentlessly as an undercover spy. It'll be there lurking at the back of your mind during every conversation you have, every email you

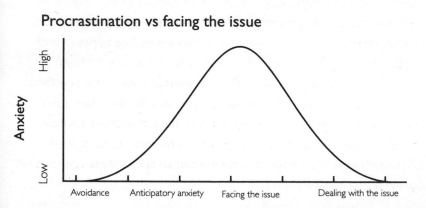

Procrastination vs facing the issue

write, every glass of wine you glug. This can become so stressful that
the avoidance itself becomes something to worry about too. Now
you're not only avoiding the situation, but your thoughts and your
guilt. Avoidance takes up a lot of time and energy and can make other
totally non-related tasks seem more arduous. You'll also probably notice
yourself becoming irritable and defensive about things because you're
on edge.

Your mind works in annoying ways. When you're trying not to
think about something, it's usually the only thing you can think about.
It's like the pink elephant again – trying not to think about it means
you are thinking about it. Your thoughts concerning it actually increase.

Ⓢ Train of thought

Instead of trying to push your worries about the issue out of your
mind, just let them come ... and then let them go. Imagine each
thought about the situation you're avoiding is a high-speed train. Next
time one clatters into your head, look at it, acknowledge it ... and then
don't get on the train. Let it whizz off without you. Don't engage with
the thought.

If you practise this with whatever visual imagery works for you (you
could send the thought off on a leaf floating on a stream), then you'll
notice a marked decline in the frequency of these thoughts over time
and even when they do appear they won't bother you as much. The
key thing is to acknowledge the thought and accept it's there and then
choose not to engage with it.

Facing your fears

Changing how you act when confronted with an intimidating task is integral to becoming calmer and less stressed. When you're avoiding something you don't have a clear idea of what you're dealing with which tricks your mind into making it worse than it is, which in turn makes you think you can't cope. At least if you try to deal with it you're giving yourself a fair shot.

It's time to bite the bullet. Once you actually start facing things you'll soon realise they're far more manageable than you anticipated – or they're hard, but still easier than they would have been tomorrow or the day after or the month after that.

You have to promise yourself that, having made a start, you're not going to abandon things half way through otherwise you're not giving yourself a chance at succeeding and won't ever have an opportunity to disprove your fears about how you can cope.

Ⓢ Lists, glorious lists

+ Make a list of things you're avoiding
+ Order the list with either the easiest stuff first through to the hardest, or the most enjoyable to the most horrible (often the same thing)
+ Pick the easiest or most enjoyable thing on the list to start with and do something about it. Starting easy will give you motivation to face the harder things – the things you're dreading. You'll gain confidence and feel in a better position to tackle the bigger tasks
+ If you have one massive thing that you're putting off, work through it by breaking it down into smaller parts (see the mountain to

molehill technique in Chapter 5). When there's one big task looming over you it can feel overwhelming and you can end up not starting at all. Starting is often the hardest bit and once you've done that you'll feel less guilty – and less stressed – about your avoidance tendencies

If the thought of addressing the bigger tasks is terrifying the steps opposite will help them feel more manageable:

1 Picture yourself in the situation or dealing with the problem, but picture the best, most confident version of yourself you can. It's you, but on your best ever day.

2 Imagine the event or issue doesn't stress you out at all and that you haven't been putting it off. You're just dealing with it and doing what you need to.

3 How would this uber efficient and confident you deal with it? What would you do? What solutions would you come up with? Are there any potential obstacles? If so, how would you get over them?

4 Okay, this bit may sound weird, but go with it: picture what you're wearing, how you hold yourself, the tone of your voice and what you can see and hear around you. Picture where you are, what kind of room you're in.

5 Now imagine a really insecure version of you walks in – the version that you see yourself as now. What does this version think about the

task? 'It's too hard. We don't have enough time.' What would the confident you say in reply? What positive advice do they have to give? Can they confront and challenge the negative or anxious predictions of the fearful you? (Go through Chapter 8 and re-read some of the strategies on thought challenging.) No doubt the confident you will give the timid one a piece of their mind.

6 Go through this imagined scenario in your head a few times until it doesn't seem so ridiculous. Often we just need to tell ourselves to snap out of something. It doesn't matter how many times anyone else says it, it needs to come from us.

7 Now follow your own advice and get on with it. The confident you clearly addressed the potential problems and started finding solutions so there should be no nasty surprises.

8 If this doesn't work for you get a friend or partner to sit with you while you explain exactly how you're going to start facing this situation or problem. Often hearing yourself describe a plan out loud can give you the kick up the backside you need to actually get on with it. And, don't forget, just by doing this you're already starting to face the issue, rather than avoiding it – and that's a big deal.

Dealing with anticipatory anxiety

Once you've ticked off some of the things on your to-do list and have reined in your addiction to procrastination, it's time to address the realities of the situation so that when you come across an issue in the

What are/were you avoiding?	What was the feared outcome?	How likely did it feel (0 = not very likely, 10 = inevitable)	What was the actual outcome?	Was it better or worse than predicted?	How did you cope?
Starting a piece of important work	That it wouldn't be good enough	9	My boss thought there were some good suggestions in it	Much better	Actually okay
Going to see friends	I won't have a good time because I feel so anxious	7	Met them and had a great time. It took my mind off my anxiety	Much better	Really well
Taking my driving theory exam	I'm going to fail as I haven't done enough revision	10	I did fail, but only by two marks. If I actually do some revision, I'll pass easily next time	The same	Even though I didn't pass, it wasn't as big a deal as I thought it would be
Calling to make a doctor's appointment	I don't want to ring in case I have to explain why I need to see the doctor	7	I called and they asked me some subtle questions that didn't embarrass me	Better than expected	Really well

future you'll be far less likely to file it away under 'avoid at all costs'.

As we've already discussed, our minds get a kick out of making us believe all sorts of weird and warped things are going to happen when we're feeling anxious. We anticipate outcomes that are massively unrealistic. However, now you've faced some of your fears you should know first-hand that these things are hardly ever as bad as they seem.

Fill out the table opposite based upon some of the things you ticked off on the 'facing your fears' list. We tend not to pay as much attention to actual outcomes as we do to feared outcomes, especially when things turn out okay in the end. We'll dwell on times when things went wrong, not when they went well. Logging what actually happens will make you more likely to remember positive outcomes the next time you're struggling and need some motivation.

You can use this on a day-to-day basis, making notes of any stresses that you're avoiding when they occur and updating the column detailing how you coped. Even if the feared outcome does happen the chances are you'll cope really well and gain confidence.

How you feel before you start facing the issue or dealing with a situation won't have any bearing on how you feel when you're finished. As we've said, the best predictor of future behaviour is past behaviour – so the more often you behave in new, positive ways the more likely you are to keep repeating these new behaviours and the more your confidence will grow. If you're used to procrastinating then you will continue to do so … unless you choose to change.

Thoughts to take away

✓ Facing your fears and dealing with problems head-on will build your confidence and convince your sceptical brain that you can do things and you can cope

✓ By just starting something you've put off, or by facing something you've been avoiding, your anxiety and guilt levels will drop

✓ The outcomes of events are never as bad as our anxious mind predicts them to be. Prove this to yourself by addressing stuff you've been putting off

10

How to Stay Calm

Now you have some strategies locked down to help you get through the worst of those panicky moments, it's time to concentrate on more general things you can do to stay zen-like all day every day.

Get healthy

Shock, horror – being healthy is good for you! Yeah, we know this isn't news, but we also know a puff-pastry pie can be a lot more appetising than a salad. There are some really basic facts about ourselves, as humans, that we tend to ignore. In today's crazy 'do-everything-this-second-and-get-your-perks-where-you-can' society it's easy to put stuff off, forget about it, or go for the quick fix. And that isn't only about diet, it's about everything. We eat quickly, we speak quickly, we make and lose friends quickly, we work quickly. When everything's go, go, go, we want to feel good now and thinking about the future is boring. We forget that quick-fixes are always a false economy (like painting over damp or cutting your hair yourself after a few margaritas).

When you're stressed and feeling down it's easy to fall back on bad habits to give yourself a quick boost – comfort eating, avoidance, drink and drugs, etc. They may deliver a bit of respite, but it's always short-lived. Then there's the guilt to deal with afterwards as well as the

The 80:20 rule

Apply the 80:20 rule when it comes to your life. Aim to live well 80 per cent of the time and allow yourself 20 per cent worth of slack. No one's perfect and being healthy shouldn't ever become something else to stress about. Incorporating the suggestions here into your week will make a big difference to how you feel about yourself and how your life's going.

anxiety you already had. Having a healthy lifestyle is such an easy and quick way to feel calmer.

Your stress resistance levels will be hugely boosted by munching healthy foods, curbing excessive drinking, not swigging too much coffee and trying to get enough sleep. But it's not all about your physical health, you can make your mind healthier by taking time out, slowing down, talking about how you feel and seeing your mates. All things that can be easily sacrificed when you're feeling grim.

Ⓢ Eat stress-busting foods

A healthy diet can counteract the impact of stress, improve your immune system and lower blood pressure. Everybody's different and what people like to eat and what they can eat while maintaining a healthy weight varies hugely from person to person – but there are some undeniable facts about certain foods that make them pretty invaluable for reducing stress:

✦ Foods rich in vitamin C such as thyme, parsley, broccoli, cauliflower and kiwis help return blood pressure and cortisol (which is released during the fight or flight response) to normal levels. If your body is feeling calmer your head will soon follow

✦ Magnesium, found in dried apricots and green leafy vegetables like spinach is integral to a healthy body. It helps regularise your blood pressure, helps you sleep, enhances circulation, prevents osteoporosis, boosts your metabolism, and eases muscle aches and spasms. Symptoms of magnesium deficiency include heart flutters, migraines, twitches and muscle cramps. Drinking too much coffee, eating foods rich in sugar and wolfing too many processed ready-meals can all deplete your magnesium levels. You can get magnesium supplements, but speak to the pharmacist about the right dosage for you

+ Porridge and bananas both contain serotonin – a feel-good calming hormone

+ Fish, such as salmon and tuna, contain omega-3 fatty acids which can prevent surges in stress hormones adrenaline and cortisol. It can also protect against depression and PMS

+ Nuts are packed with vitamins. Almonds contain vitamins B and E, which help boost your immune system and are a good source of healthy fats

+ Avocados and bananas contain potassium, which lowers blood pressure

⑤ Exercise

Exercise is not only an excellent distraction from stress, working up a sweat and getting your blood pumping (for reasons other than fight or flight) is also a great way of releasing pent-up frustrations and aggression. When you exercise your body works off the biochemical and physical changes that occur in the body during stress, giving you a boost by releasing endorphins that naturally make you feel good. It also helps to regulate blood pressure and is good for your heart.

If you're not used to exercising start slowly – perhaps visit a gym and speak to a personal trainer about what would be best for you or chat to your GP.

Make sure you do something you enjoy. If you hate jogging and haven't broken a sweat in years, promising yourself and everyone who'll listen that you're going to run a marathon is only going to end in self-recrimination when you can't. By making realistic goals and doing activities you actually enjoy such as walking, swimming or dancing, you're more likely to stick to a routine.

Ⓢ Cut down (or cut out) drink, drugs, nicotine and caffeine

It's all fun and games until your heart starts fluttering and your hands start shaking. Drink, drugs, cigarettes and caffeine are the very definition of a quick fix and they only add to your problems in the long-term when you're prone to stress (yep, even caffeine). Caffeine and nicotine are stimulants (as are some recreational drugs) and so they mimic the fight or flight response – the physical symptoms of anxiety. Too much and you'll be buzzing which in the short-term might feel great, but as with any high there's always the inevitable crash, which kicks you in the teeth. Also, if you're in fight or flight mode and then have an espresso or a fizzy drink (many of which contain caffeine) your body won't know how to deal with it. You'll just exacerbate the symptoms you're already experiencing.

Alcohol is a depressant. It slows down your breathing and reaction times and relaxes your muscles. Everyone has different tolerance levels and you'll no doubt know your own, so just be aware that dealing with a hangover when you're stressed isn't great. You'll trigger the morning-after guilt and paranoia cycles which in turn will trigger the fight or flight response.

Basically the rule is: know your limits. Having a drink or a coffee can be hugely calming when feeling stressed – and the very act of pouring yourself a drink can be relaxing. The problems come when you have too much or have them at the wrong time and then have to think about the repercussions. We don't want to sound like the grumpy gran at a party, but these are really simple ways of not giving yourself additional things to worry about.

⑤ Get enough sleep

We can't over-emphasise the importance of sleep to feeling calm (so much so that we've written a whole book on the subject, *This Book Will Make You Sleep*). Lack of sleep is a common symptom of stress and anxiety. If you're having trouble sleeping it's important to try and keep to a routine, going to bed at a similar time each day and waking up at the same time so your body knows when to expect sleep. Also avoid taking naps and be wary of too much caffeine, alcohol and nicotine as this will disrupt your sleep cycle.

There are some practical things you can do to improve your sleeping habits. A simple place to start is to improve where you sleep. Making the environment that you rest in inviting, welcoming and calming is essential to getting into the right mindset to sleep. Lots of this will depend on your own personal preferences and everyone is different, but making your room a relaxing place to be is a good place to start. Things to consider:

✦ Comfort. Is your bed too soft or too hard?
✦ Light. It needs to be as dark as possible as we're programmed to wake when it's light outside. Consider investing in blackout blinds or an eye mask if your room isn't dark enough
✦ Noise. Even if you think you can sleep through a typhoon when

you're stressed you'll be more sensitive to distractions – and noise serves as one of the biggest. Invest in earplugs if your room is too noisy

+ Temperature and ventilation. If you're too hot it'll be very hard to drop off. A cooler room is more conducive to sleep, but make sure you're not too cold

Slow down
Mentally

Everyone has a smart phone, an iPad, a Blackberry, an MP3 player or all of the above nowadays. We're instantly accessible and there's an expectation that we should be. Being constantly online or plugged into social media can be reassuring, making us feel connected, up-to-date and even giving us a feeling of validation when people reply or 'like' something we've posted.

However, technology overload has a lot to answer for where stress is concerned. (We're willing to bet the first thing you did this morning, before you even stretched, was check your phone. No? Good for you – but you'll be in the minority.) We're never unconnected unless we make a concerted effort to be and then we can worry about the consequences of being cut adrift from our cyber life.

If this sounds like you, start taking notice of how long you spend online or with a gadget in your hand. Often we just reach for our phone on autopilot because we're bored. Don't. Give yourself definite switch-off times. For example, tell yourself you're not allowed to look at your phone before you leave the house in the morning. You'll probably be amazed at how alien this feels and how often you reach for it automatically. We promise that giving yourself an hour off now and then will give your mind some breathing space.

Physically

Rushing everywhere is part of everyday life, but it's stressful. When you're rushing it gives your body the impression that you're late which will make you feel anxious. There isn't a single situation we can think of (feel free to tell us otherwise) when being late isn't stressful. (If you're being fashionably late you're not actually late, see?) Giving yourself an extra five minutes for everything will make you physically slow down which will mean you don't have to barge people out of your way or juggle four bags while leaping up flights of stairs. Everything is easier if you give yourself more time.

Just walking rather than trotting will give you an appearance of calmness – which is contagious. You'll appear more in control to others as well as yourself.

Focusing on one thing at a time is a guaranteed way to slow yourself down physically and mentally. Don't multi-task and you'll automatically feel calmer.

❺ Talk about things

It's essential to talk. Keeping your emotions bottled up will only lead to more stress, worry and anxiety and possibly an explosion of some sort.

Speaking to people (be it colleagues, friends, family or a friendly stranger on the bus) can help you to reflect on what's happened and to get a different perspective, advice and support. Sometimes just talking something through out loud can give you distance and help you to see things maybe aren't as bad as you'd built them up to be. Old clichés usually have some basis in truth and 'a problem shared is a problem halved' is a good example of this. While the issue won't just disappear by you speaking about it, feeling as if you've got allies will make whatever you're facing automatically less intimidating.

While we're not suggesting ranting and raving about every little thing, avoiding discussing issues that are genuinely concerning you can lead to feelings of frustration, helplessness and anger. Chatting about things lifts a burden, can clear up misunderstandings, create solutions and make you feel less alone.

⑤ See the funny side

Laughter really is the best medicine for pretty much anything. Researchers at Oxford University discovered laughing causes the body to release endorphins that act as natural painkillers, so you honestly do feel better after a good guffaw. The research group was split into two: one was made to watch fifteen minutes of so-called 'boring' programmes (such as golf tournaments – seriously) while the other watched fifteen minutes of comedy shows. Scientists found that the people who had recently experienced belly laughs were able to withstand 10 per cent more pain than they had done before watching the shows, while the other group were less able to bear pain.

So there you have it – laughing is good for you. You'll feel physically able to cope with more and become calmer. You'll give your mind a rest from the stress, feel less tense and get a better perspective on what's actually going on.

Ⓢ Avoid unnecessary conflict

Anger and conflict can often become by-products of stress as we're more easily irritated and frustrated. For example, when you're driving and you're stressed you're more likely to shout at other drivers and hate the journey. Anger is like Velcro – it sticks to you and is hard to get off. And once you're a little bit narked, even small things can set you off.

Anger can be useful in small amounts as it can make you stick up for yourself and it can be a good motivator. However, if you're feeling irritable all the time you'll become more negative, less confident and generally pretty hard to be around.

When you're next feeling angry take five deep breaths before reacting. Firing off retorts over email or in person will only aggravate the situation and you. Don't look for a fight. There's no point in becoming aggressive – the only person who loses is you. Whatever has happened and however wronged you feel, everything will be more manageable if you take five deep breaths (counting them down as you do) and, if possible, remove yourself from the situation for several minutes. This will slow your heart rate and make you feel more in control. When you've calmed down reassess the situation. Anger can make you biased so you'll see things in black and white and ignore all shades of grey. The only way to deal with this is not to make any snap judgements as you're not seeing things clearly. If you still feel a robust response is necessary then you can write that email or speak to the person in question, but don't do it in the heat of the moment when your judgement is clouded.

⑤ Make time for friends and family

The importance of social support cannot be underestimated. While you may not feel like going out, seeing people will take your mind off things and remind you of life outside of your worries.

Next steps ...

Putting all of these strategies into practice will ensure you can keep a calm and collected demeanour no matter what's happening, making everything more manageable. Making small alterations to your day-to-day life will add up to one big change. You'll feel more in control, more content and happier, which will ensure you're better able to face stress head-on.

Thoughts to take away

✓ Staying healthy by exercising and watching your diet will make you feel better able to face problems

✓ Slowing down both physically and mentally will give your mind a much needed break

✓ Communication and social support are essential no matter what's going on in your life

A final message

Congratulations! You've made it to the final chapter, hopefully feeling much calmer than you did when you first picked up the book. The fact that you've taken action and chosen not to accept stress and anxiety as permanent fixtures in your life is something you should be very proud of.

If you feel more confident in your ability to cope with whatever life throws at you then please take a moment to pat yourself on the back, crack open some fizz or do a little jig. Making these changes will have been – and will continue to be – hard, and recognising how far you've come is really important. Don't underestimate what you've achieved – feeling even just a tiny bit calmer is something to be celebrated.

As a means to measure how far you've come please answer the following questions:

1 After reading the book – how do you feel?
  A The same – no change
  B A smidgen better – starting to think this all through
  C Better – putting in place improvements
  D Amazing – transformed

If you answered option A did you really invest all your energy into the strategies? Are you willing to try them again? If you are still having difficulties and the book hasn't helped you as much as you'd hoped, then we suggest speaking to your GP who should be able to recommend further treatment. There are some useful resources and websites at the back of the book.

If you answered B–D then we're very chuffed for you and things can only get better from here if you keep putting what you've learned into practice.

2 **Which specific skills and strategies did you find particularly helpful?** Make sure you keep practising them until they become second nature.

3 **Which of the 'takeaways' listed at the bottom of all the chapters particularly struck a chord?** Write them down on a notepad or in your diary so every time you need a pick-me-up, or alternatively a kick up the arse you can flick through and motivate yourself.

4 **What support network do you have to help you maintain what you've learned?** Consider telling family and friends what you're doing, if you haven't already. Their encouragement will be invaluable and motivational and just saying things out loud can help, giving you a bit of distance from the problem and some clarity.

5 **What possible obstacles do you see in the future that might throw you off course?** Write them down and then work through any possible solutions.

6 **Are you going to stop avoiding problems and putting off facing issues and start thinking about ways to deal with them?**

7 **Are you going to disregard 'what ifs' and any worries you can't control and instead focus only on the problems that you can influence?**

8 **Are you going to look for both the positives and the negatives in all situations?**

9 **Go through the tick list of symptoms in Chapter 2 again. Are there many changes for the better?**

10 When are you going to start thinking differently?

A I already have

B Today

C Tomorrow

D Next week

E Next year

F I don't care

The point of these questions isn't to harass you or make you feel anxious and there are no right or wrong answers. This is a chance to assess how you feel now and if there are any specific areas you want to concentrate on. You have the tools to cope with stress better – how you use them is up to you. If you're excited about making changes then we salute you. It's really hard, but very rewarding. And it works.

If there are some bits of the book that you haven't tackled yet, don't worry. Go back and try again, reminding yourself what you're meant to be doing and why. It's incredibly difficult to change your behaviour and the way you think, especially when habits have been built up over years and years. However, it is possible. Often just considering doing things differently is the hardest bit – and you've got past that stage by reading this book! Tell yourself you'll give everything a try and see how it goes. Don't put undue pressure on yourself to change overnight. These things take time, but it's time well spent. Unfortunately, you can't get rid of stress and anxiety completely, they're a natural part of life – but they shouldn't rule your life.

Now that you're feeling a bit better in the here and now you can start planning for the future. We want you to identify goals that you can take forward to give you a sense of direction and hope, achievement and fulfilment. It's like a day-to-day to-do list, but on a bigger and grander scale. You can plan both short-term, medium-term and long-term goals. Start thinking about what you want to be doing next week, month, year and how you want to be feeling. Thinking about what you want to do next and actually making the plan means you're much more likely to achieve it. Also assess which strategies you particularly liked and plan how you're going to keep using them and how they'll help you to achieve your goals. As a way to measure your progress, you could make a date to re-read the book in two months or a year's time to evaluate how differently you feel next time around and to keep all the ideas fresh in your head. Also, keep flicking through your notebook. It'll remind you of how you coped previously and also that you did cope previously. Never forget that past behaviour is the best predicator of future events. You've experienced stress and anxiety before and got through it so you will again.

This is all about making changes that last. Of course there'll be times when you slip up, but these strategies and techniques will continue to work for you if you keep using them. Build them seamlessly into your life and use these principles to guide you going forward so that you can feel happier and calmer.

Remember: stress doesn't have to control you – you can and will regain and maintain control of your life. You're well on your way to feeling happier, calmer and confident in your ability to cope with whatever comes your way.

Good luck!

Further reading

Helen Kennerly, *Overcoming Anxiety* (London, Constable & Robinson, 2009)

Lee Bronson and Gilliant Todd, *Overcoming Stress* (London, Constable & Robinson, 2009)

Robert Leahy, *The Worry Cure* (London, Piatkus, 2008)

Dennis Greenberg and Christine Padesky, *Mind Over Mood: A Cognitive Treatment Manual for Clients* (New York, Guilford Press, 1995)

Useful websites

MIND, The National Association for Mental Health: www.mind.org.uk

Time to Change: www.time-to-change.org.uk

Anxiety UK: www.anxietyuk.org.uk

Mood Gym: https:moodgym.anu.edu.au

Living Life to the Full: www.llttf.com

The Centre for Clinical Interventions: www.cci.health.wa.gov.au/resources

The Mental Health Foundation: www.mentalhealth.org.uk

The American Mental Health Foundation: americanmentalhealthfoundation.org

The Beck Institute: www.beckinstitute.org

Cruse Bereavement Care: www.cruse.org.uk

Relate: www.relate.org.uk/home/index.html

Frank: friendly confidential drugs advice: www.talktofrank.com

Alcohol Concern: www.alcoholconcern.org.uk

The British Psychological Society: www.bps.org.uk

The British Association for Behavioural & Cognitive Psychotherapy: www.babcp.com

Samaritans: www.samaritans.org

Acknowledgements

Thanks to all the people who believed in these books and helped to make them happen. Big thanks to our wonderful families, particularly Ben, Jack, Max and Edie. Also to our agent Jane Graham Maw for brilliant advice, our editor Kerry Enzor for her contagious enthusiasm and Peggy Sadler for her unsurpassed design skills. Jessamy would also like to thank the psychologists, health professionals and patients who have educated, supported and inspired her.